PENGUIN CANADA

A LITTLE BOOK OF FACTS
ABOUT A REALLY BIG COUNTRY

"Curious fun" are words used by essayist and travel writer Jan Morris to describe the writings of JOHN ROBERT COLOMBO. The author, compiler, editor, or translator of over 180 books, Colombo has an insatiable curiosity for bits of lore and learning that shed light on what it means to be a Canadian and, hence, what it means to be a reflective person and thoughtful citizen of the world. Recent publications of his include *The Penguin Treasury of Popular Canadian Poems and Songs* and *The Penguin Dictionary of Popular Canadian Quotations*. He holds an honorary doctorate from York University and is a Member of the Order of Canada.

Also by John Robert Colombo

The Penguin Book of Canadian Jokes

The Penguin Book of More Canadian Jokes

The Penguin Treasury of Popular Canadian Poems and Songs

The Penguin Dictionary of Popular Canadian Quotations

A Little Book of Facts About a Really Big Country

John Robert Colombo

PENGUIN
CANADA

PENGUIN CANADA

Published by the Penguin Group

Penguin Group (Canada), 90 Eglinton Avenue East, Suite 700, Toronto, Ontario, Canada M4P 2Y3
(a division of Pearson Canada Inc.)

Penguin Group (USA) Inc., 375 Hudson Street, New York, New York 10014, U.S.A.
Penguin Books Ltd, 80 Strand, London WC2R 0RL, England
Penguin Ireland, 25 St Stephen's Green, Dublin 2, Ireland (a division of Penguin Books Ltd)
Penguin Group (Australia), 250 Camberwell Road, Camberwell, Victoria 3124, Australia
(a division of Pearson Australia Group Pty Ltd)
Penguin Books India Pvt Ltd, 11 Community Centre, Panchsheel Park, New Delhi – 110 017, India
Penguin Group (NZ), cnr Airborne and Rosedale Roads, Albany, Auckland 1310, New Zealand
(a division of Pearson New Zealand Ltd)
Penguin Books (South Africa) (Pty) Ltd, 24 Sturdee Avenue, Rosebank, Johannesburg 2196, South Africa

Penguin Books Ltd, Registered Offices: 80 Strand, London WC2R 0RL, England

First published 2007

1 2 3 4 5 6 7 8 9 10   (WEB)

Copyright © John Robert Colombo, 2007

*Publisher's note: This book is a work of fiction. Names, characters, places and incidents
either are the product of the author's imagination or are used fictitiously, and any
resemblance to actual persons living or dead, events, or locales is entirely coincidental.*

Manufactured in Canada.

Library and Archives Canada Cataloguing in Publication data available upon request.

ISBN-13: 978-0-14-305368-2
ISBN-10: 0-14-305368-X

Visit the Penguin Group (Canada) website at **www.penguin.ca**

Special and corporate bulk purchase rates available; please see
www.penguin.ca/corporatesales or call 1-800-810-3104, ext. 477 or 474

Contents

Preface

―――― ―― ―― ―― ―― ――

This little book brims over with interesting and important facts and fancies about a really big country.

Interesting facts are little-known but odd details about our country and its people. Important facts are hard-nosed details about its geography, history, demographics, and politics. Fancies are trivia, minutiae, and other little treasures that enliven one's day.

Knowing interesting and important facts and fancies about one's native land broadens one's appreciation of that land and deepens one's understanding of himself or herself. A maxim of mine has always been "Canada only needs to be known in order to be great." National knowledge is part of self-knowledge. So a really big country should really broaden and deepen one's appreciation of life in general.

The wonders of Canada are "hidden in wonder," wrote one of our poets. They are hidden because the country is so huge that people are inclined to get lost in it. Too often we think in municipal, provincial, or regional terms; instead, we should embrace the whole and spend some time thinking nationally. After all, the rest of the world sees us this way, and it sees us as an unusual and lucky country.

I like to call the contents of this collection "facts with fun," but the fun I have in mind is "deep fun." It is deep because it is informative and challenging, more like a quiz than a questionnaire or checklist; it is not a waste of time, and hardly of ephemeral interest.

Let me illustrate what I mean by way of an ongoing argument that I have with my friend Simson Najovits. I do not see Simson very often because I live in Toronto and he lives in Paris, but we do meet about every 10 years, and once a month we exchange emails. Born in Montreal in the early 1940s, he graduated from Sir George Williams College (today's Concordia University), and shortly after began to write serious short stories and publish them. Then he decided Canada was not for him. Since he spoke excellent French and appreciated the lifestyle of the Parisians, he settled in Paris, worked as a radio broadcaster for the French network, and launched a writing career, producing, among other works, a well-regarded, two-volume history of ancient Egypt.

In correspondence and in person, he made Canada's failings apparent. He did so more in regret than in anger. He derided Canada for its failings, assessing everything from the vantage point of the City of Light. For decades I would concede his points: Canada is the world's bore, Canadian culture is not a mature culture, Canada does not pull its weight on the international scene, and so on.

Then one day I decided enough was enough, so I went on the offensive. "Simson," I told him, "you are right to deride our political correctness; our inept Mounties; our lacklustre politicians; our treatment of the Aboriginals and their unsettled land claims; English Canada's lack of understanding of Quebec; our preoccupation with such notions as 'one Canada,' 'special status,' 'distinct society,' and now 'nation within nation'; our obsession with the game of hockey and our acceptance of violence on ice; our church-basement moralizing; and all the rest. I grant those irritations.

"But, Simson, what you are doing is overlooking our splendid achievements, perhaps because you are unfamiliar with them. You never say a word about these, and these are what excite me about the country. It is true that not every Canadian is knowledgeable about them, but in my books and talks I have always tried to draw attention to our collective and individual accomplishments."

"What do you have in mind?" he asked.

"Let me list more than a dozen of them. I could double or triple that number, but I will constrain myself. In no particular order, here they are ... Let me begin with three world-recognized institutions: the Pugwash conferences for scientists during the Cold War, the Antigonish (co-operative) movements for the underdeveloped world, and the Greenpeace movement for the developed world. Then there is our ongoing commitment in the world's trouble spots to peacekeeping (and now peacemaking, alas). There are government-sponsored policies of multiculturalism and bilingualism, certainly landmarks in their day.

"At home we have a prosperous country, a just society, a peaceable kingdom, a democratic government, and a way of life that is ranked among the top six—and sometimes first—by the UN's Human Development Index. We have a wonderful if underfunded health care system. Thoughtful Canadians take pride in the Crown corporations: Canadian Broadcasting Corporation, National Film Board, Canada Council, to name just a few. (To keep these in check, we harbour an accountant's grudging respect for number-crunching pressure groups such as the Fraser Institute and the C.D. Howe Institute.)

"Then there are men and women who have achieved renown, not so much as national figures but as contributors to excellence. Everyone's appreciation of the country is enriched by the creators of Eskimo sculpture and woodland Indian art. There are the 'three Canadian geniuses' (Glenn Gould, Marshall McLuhan, Northrop Frye). There are filmmakers like Norman McLaren and Denys Arcand and Deepa Mehta, directors like Robert Lepage, performers of Cirque du Soleil, writers like Alice Munro and Mavis Gallant and Robertson Davies, pop singers and comedy performers aplenty, painters like Paul-Émile Borduas and Lawren Harris, singers like Leonard Cohen, composers like R. Murray Schafer, and multi-gifted creators like Robert Bringhurst and Douglas Coupland. Then there are our scientists and our athletes. I could go on!"

"Okay," Simson protested. "I give up. These *are* outstanding achievements and achievers—for a country that is young and underpopulated and culturally undeveloped. I felt I could develop no further—no deeper—as a writer and as a person in Canada. So I opted to live abroad. As did some of our celebrated writers and painters: Mavis Gallant, Mordecai Richler, Paul-Émile Borduas, Nancy Huston …"

"You are wrong about the country being young and underpopulated. As a country, Canada is one of the oldest of the world's democracies, and its confederal form of government has influenced many other countries' constitution. Canada should not be described as underpopulated. Of the 195 nations, with populations ranging from China's 1.3 billion teeming mass to Vatican City's 932 lonely souls, Canada ranks about number 35.

By the same token, it is hardly undeveloped, though there are many critics at home and abroad who feel the country's cultural industries are underdeveloped and so have yet to meet their potential. Opportunities and challenges, as businessmen say."

"I have problems with the official aspects of bilingualism and multiculturalism; there is no joy there," complained Simson.

"So do I," I said. "No government policy or program lasts more than two decades without doing some harm. We have had official multiculturalism since the late 1960s. We should redefine it to reflect current national needs and international realities, and perhaps rename the relevant parts of the policy 'polyculturalism.' As for official bilingualism, to the degree that it supplies federal government services in both official languages 'where numbers warrant,' it is popular with reasonable people, and even with members of the separatist-minded Bloc Québécois."

Simson continued, "Thomas Bernhard, the Austrian novelist, hit the nail on the head when he referred to Glenn Gould as one of those 'Canadian Americans.' And Northrop Frye was right when he talked about 'our famous problem of identity' and asked, 'Where is here?' The only Canadian region I have ever experienced as distinctively different from the American is northern Canada, and even that is probably no longer the case."

"You're more right than wrong, but—"

"I give up!" exclaimed Simson, to my surprise. I think my vigorous rather than rigorous defence of Canadian principles (in the face sometimes of Canadian realities) amused him. I had worried that they would irritate him. But he rose into the stratosphere of sophistication—perhaps France does this to the spirit of man—and delivered a definitive pronouncement: "I have reserved a table for us for dinner tonight at eight o'clock at La Coupole in Montparnasse. When Canada produces a brasserie as fine as La Coupole, I will concede all your points, confess my sins, and return to Montreal for my retirement."

So much for going on the offensive with Simson. He wins the last point: While we have a handful of fine restaurants in our major cities, there is not one of them in the league of La Coupole, with its long and illustrious history and its fine food. That is something for our future.

IT IS A PECULIARITY of this book that it makes light of some of the standard icons, emblems, and symbols of sovereignty. For instance, there are no references at all to the fleur-de-lys, the floral emblem of the French in Canada, or to the beaver, the ever-busy rodent that for centuries has epitomized the industry of the inhabitants of the land. Indeed, the sole reference to the Maple Leaf that makes its appearance is in a section devoted to the name of the Toronto Maple Leafs. Flag-waving was fine for yesterday. Today and tomorrow we need to do more: to recognize and celebrate quality of life, achievement, excellence, intelligence, and imagination. It is not sufficient to be Canadians: Let's be terrific people as well.

There are quirky items in these pages, as well as references to achievements everyone knows about, because the selection is at once personal and impersonal. Using a sports metaphor, I have kept my eye on the big field but, from time to time, I have been distracted by the brilliance of individual plays. But that is okay by me because I see the country as (surprise!) a

mosaic of magical moments: a patchwork quilt, a box of allsorts, a reflection of the pattern of the world itself. It was Montreal poet and scholar
F.R. Scott who noted that we are "hidden in wonder" and that we grow
"through enlargement of wonder." His observation is no less true today
than the day in 1954 when he made it, in a poem titled "A Grain of Rice."
So here are some wonders in a little book for a great big wonderful
country.

A
Little Book of Facts
about a
Really Big
Country

Where We Are

Hail!

Here are greetings in both official languages and in two Native tongues, as well as in Esperanto. Match the words of greeting with their respective languages.

1. Ahneen!
2. Ai!
3. Hello!
4. Salut!
5. Saluton!

a. Algonquian
b. English
c. Esperanto
d. French
e. Inuktitut

ANSWERS:
1. a Cree greeting; 2. e. "Hi!" in Inuktitut, the language of the Inuit of northern Quebec;
3. b. English; 4. d. French; 5. c. Esperanto, artificial world language.

Big country

This may be a little book, with only 176 pages, but Canada is a great *big* country:

Land: 9,093,507 square kilometres
Water: 891,163 square kilometres
Total: 9,984,670 square kilometres

So, our country is almost 10 million square kilometres. A little less than 10 percent of it is covered in water—liquid overlay.

First? Second?

Ours is the largest country in the Western Hemisphere, and the second largest country in the Northern Hemisphere—first in size is Russia; third in size is China. The United States comes fourth. We are in the large league.

Provinces and territories

Are you able to cite the Canadian provinces and territories in order of decreasing size? Areas in square kilometres appear in the left-hand column. Match the areas with the provinces and territories, listed below.

1.	1,936,113	a.	Alberta
2.	1,183,085	b.	British Columbia
3.	1,365,128	c.	Newfoundland and Labrador
4.	925,186	d.	New Brunswick
5.	917,741	e.	Nova Scotia
6.	642,317	f.	Manitoba
7.	591,670	g.	Northwest Territories
8.	553,556	h.	Nunavut
9.	474,391	i.	Ontario
10.	373,872	j.	Prince Edward Island
11.	74,450	k.	Quebec
12.	53,338	l.	Saskatchewan
13.	5660	m.	Yukon Territory

ANSWERS:
1. h; 2. g; 3. k; 4. b; 5. i; 6. a; 7. l; 8. f; 9. m; 10. c; 11. d; 12. e; 13. j.

Provinces and states

Are the following statements true or false? Answer them, and then check a map of North America.

1. British Columbia touches both Alaska and Idaho.   T ☐   F ☐

2. Alberta touches both Idaho and Montana.   T ☐   F ☐

3. Saskatchewan touches both Montana and North Dakota.   T ☐   F ☐

4. Manitoba touches both North Dakota and Minnesota.   T ☐   F ☐

5. Ontario touches both Wisconsin and Pennsylvania.   T ☐   F ☐

6. Quebec touches both New York State and Massachusetts.   T ☐   F ☐

7. New Brunswick touches both Maine and New Hampshire.   T ☐   F ☐

8. Nova Scotia touches both New Brunswick and Maine.   T ☐   F ☐

ANSWERS:
1. True; 2. False; 3. True; 4. True; 5. False; 6. False; 7. False; 8. False.

Highest mountain

What is the name of the highest mountain in the country? (Clue: It is located in Yukon Territory.)

ANSWER:
The highest mountain is Mt. Logan, Yukon Territory. Rising 5959 metres, it is almost 12 times the height of Toronto's CN Tower.

The Great Lakes

The Great Lakes form the largest body of fresh water in the world. Their total area covers 244,160 square kilometres. The "great five" are Lakes Huron, Ontario, Michigan, Erie, and Superior. Georgian Bay is also enormous, so it is sometimes referred to as "the sixth" Great Lake.

Could Prince Edward Island fit into the area occupied by Lake Ontario?

Thomas D'Arcy McGee once said that someone should take Prince Edward Island and drop it into Lake Ontario. As a future Father of Confederation, McGee had in mind the reluctance of Islanders to join Confederation.

The island's area is 5660 square kilometres. The lake covers 19,555 square kilometres. This means three P.E.I.s could fit into Lake Ontario, with a little room left over.

Longest rivers

Here's a difficult assignment. The first list contains the names of the country's six longest rivers. Match each river with its length, listed below.

1. Columbia River
2. Mackenzie River
3. Nelson River
4. St. Lawrence River
5. Saskatchewan River
6. Yukon River

a. 4241 kilometres
b. 3185 kilometres
c. 3058 kilometres
d. 2575 kilometres
e. 2000 kilometres
f. 1939 kilometres

Bonus questions:

The total length of these six rivers is 16,998 kilometres.

1. Is the total length greater than or lesser than the sum of the greatest distances across the country east and west and across the country north and south?
2. Is the total length of these rivers approximately twice the length of Canada's borders with the United States?

ANSWERS:
1. e; 2. a; 3. d; 4. c; 5. f; 6. b. The total length of these six rivers is 16,998 kilometres.

BONUS ANSWERS:
1. The greatest distance east to west is 5514 kilometres, and the greatest distance north to south is 4634 kilometres. The sum of these is 10,148, so the combined length of the rivers is greater than the combined distances by 6850 kilometres.
2. The combined lengths of the borders with the United States (the southern border and the northern one with Alaska) is 8890 kilometres. The rivers are almost twice as long as the two borders.

Bridges

Canada boasts the world's longest bridge. It also boasts the shortest international bridge. Where are they?

ANSWER: LONGEST

The longest bridge in the world is the Confederation Bridge, at 12.9 kilometres. The S-shaped structure crosses the Northumberland Strait, joining Cape Jourimain, New Brunswick, and Borden-Carleton, Prince Edward Island. On the day it opened, in 1997, tens of thousands walked across it for free. Today's charge (two-way) is just over $40 for a motor vehicle, $8 for a cyclist, and $4 for a pedestrian—the latter two transported via a shuttle bus, as only motor vehicles are permitted to cross the bridge.

ANSWER: SHORTEST

The world's shortest international bridge is the Thousand Islands International Bridge, which spans the St. Lawrence River through the Thousand Islands, linking the province of Ontario and the state of New York.

The bridge was dedicated by Prime Minister W.L. Mackenzie King and U.S. president Roosevelt on 18 August 1938. It runs from Ivy Lea, between Brockville and Gananoque, to Collins Landing, just west of Alexandria Bay, New York. It is a complex structure of many spans. Its total length is 790 metres, just over three-quarters of a kilometre.

Directions

What is the second *most northerly province?*
The answer is counter-intuitive: The most northerly province is Quebec; the second most northerly province is Newfoundland.

What is the second *most easterly province?*
The most easterly province is Newfoundland. The second most easterly province is Quebec. (Most people think it is Nova Scotia.)

What is the second *most southerly province?*
The most southerly province is Ontario. The second most southerly province is, surprisingly, Nova Scotia. Most people would reply, mistakenly, Quebec.

Which three provincial capitals lie north of the 49th parallel?
The 49th parallel is often described as the dividing line between Canada and the United States. Yet, much of Canada lies south of the 49th parallel, including seven provincial capitals. The only three provincial capitals that lie north of the 49th parallel are Edmonton, Regina, and Winnipeg.

How many Canadians live south of the 49th parallel?

Most Canadians think that this line—the 49th parallel of latitude north of the equator—divides the North American continent into the countries of Canada and the United States. Yet, that geographical marker makes up only about one-quarter of the boundary between the two countries. Three-quarters of the country lie north of that parallel.

This fact was noted by Anne Marie Owens in "Living in a Parallel Universe," *National Post,* 17 May 2006: "The Maritime provinces, much of Quebec and most of Ontario all lie south of the 49th." She added, "The total length of the boundary between Canada and the United States is 8893 km. Of that length, only 2274 km is the 49th parallel." Cities that lie below the line include Windsor, Toronto, Niagara Falls, Halifax, and St. John's.

The population of Canada is 33 million. It is estimated that 19 million Canadians live south of the 49th parallel. Alan Rayburn, a place-name specialist, has traced the use of the phrase "the 49th parallel" back to 1714, when the Hudson's Bay Company referred to the southern limits of its land as the 49th parallel. To this day, the Canada–U.S. border is conventionally considered to be the 49th parallel—whether it is actually or not.

Are there any mnemonics for remembering places in Canada?

Yes, there are some. (Mnemonics are verbal memory aids which often make use of initial letters so chosen to form words or phrases and recall specific information.)

The mnemonics peculiar to Canada are few and far between. Perhaps Canadians have no wish to remember things! Here are the few that have been collected (lest they be lost).

ALSAMA prompts the names of the three Prairie provinces from west to east: Alberta, Saskatchewan, Manitoba.

HOMES prompts the names of the five Great Lakes in no particular order: Lake Huron, Ontario, Michigan, Erie, Superior.

"*Some men hate eating onions*" prompts the names of the Great Lakes from west to east: Superior, Michigan, Huron, Erie, Ontario.

"*Nice northern place nestled quietly over many states always befriending neighbouring Yankees*" prompts the names of the ten provinces and two territories (then two in number, since then three) from east to west.

"*No new prince*" prompts the names of the three Maritime provinces: Nova Scotia, New Brunswick, Prince Edward Island.

COSMOT prompts the names of the six Native tribes that form the Iroquois Confederacy (also called the Six Nations Confederacy): Cayuga, Oneida, Seneca, Mohawk, Onondaga, Tuscarora.

National parks

The pride of the country is its system of national parks. There are more than 40 of these federally administered parks, and they account for 3 percent of the country's land mass. There are also wonderful parks administered by the provincial governments, as well as by county and municipal authorities.

Here's a skill-testing question. Listed below are the four largest national parks. Listed below them are the locations. Can you match them?

1. Wood Buffalo
   (44,802 square kilometres)

   a. Southwest corner of Yukon Territory

2. Quttinirpaaq
   (37,775 square kilometres)

   b. Northern Baffin Island

3. Sirmilik
   (22,200 square kilometres)

   c. Northern tip of Ellesmere Island

4. Kluane
   (22,013 square kilometres)

   d. Alberta–Northwest Territories border

Bonus question:
What is the name of the smallest of the national parks?

ANSWERS:
1. d; 2. c; 3. b; 4. a.

BONUS ANSWER:
The smallest park is St. Lawrence Islands, a.k.a. Thousand Islands (8 square kilometres).

Territories

Which territory became part of Canada on 1 April 1999?

Nunavut became part of Canada on that date, which happened to be April Fool's Day. The fledgling territory, carved out of the Northwest Territories, covers 1.9 million square kilometres of the eastern Arctic. It is populated mainly by the Inuit. On some future April Fool's Day, it is expected that Denendeh will be formed in the western Arctic, the homeland of the Dene people.

Do the three territories have mottos?

No. The Northwest Territories and the Yukon Territory lack official mottos. Nunavut, the youngest of the three territories, is the only one with a motto. Its motto in Inuktitut is *Nunavut sanginivut,* which means "Nunavut our strength." The name *Nunavut* itself means "our land."

What is the difference between the badlands and the Barren Lands?

The badlands are the semi-desert region of Alberta. The tundra region of the Northwest Territories has long been known as the Barren Lands. The landforms are quite different in appearance.

Which island is Canada's most populous island?

Everyone should know that the country's largest island is Baffin Island, but the island with the largest population is a stumper. It is Île de Montréal (Montreal Island), with a population of almost two million.

Our Past

Who were the first inhabitants of the land?

The first inhabitants of the land now known as Canada were migrants from Central Asia who crossed the land bridge that once connected eastern Asia and western America. So far, the earliest signs of Asiatic settlement found in the Americas date to some thirty thousand years ago (roughly) and are located near Old Crow, Yukon Territory. Paleoanthropologists and archaeologists keep making new discoveries and hence altering their theories about early patterns of migrations, but it is safe to refer to these immigrants as Aboriginal peoples, ancestors of the citizens of Canada's First Nations.

How many words do the Inuit have for snow?

Everyone who knows the answer to this question also knows that the Inuit were once called Eskimos. But the answer to this intriguing linguistic question is not 200, 48, 27, 23, 7, 4, or zero. The answer is quite prosaic, according to linguist Geoffrey Pullum, author of *The Great Eskimo Vocabulary Hoax and Other Irreverent Essays on the Study of Language.*

Pullum observes that it is reasonable to assume that dwellers in the Far North have several words for the white stuff, just as word processors have different names for various typefaces (e.g., Times Roman, Helvetica, Cartier). The Inuit have perhaps one dozen such words, comparable to English nouns for specific types of snow and conditions, such as *avalanche, blizzard, dusting, hardpack, flurry, hail, sleet,* and *slush.*

The urban myth that the Inuit have innumerable words for snow has been traced back to 1911, when anthropologist Franz Boas observed that the Inuit used four unrelated word roots for snow. Theorists Edward Sapir and Benjamin Lee Whorf inflated the number to seven, and the popular press took it from there. Many years ago, John MacDonald of the Nunavut Research Institute observed that no matter how many words the Inuit have for snow, there is no Inuktitut word for camel.

How do the Inuit view the moon?

It may come as a surprise to learn that the Inuit traditionally held the moon to be a disk, rather than a globe or a sphere. "The moon is a thin round disk of ice which follows the sun and turns about of itself, so that it sometimes looks big and sometimes thin." So wrote Bishop Archibald L. Fleming of the Inuit perception of the moon in his 1928 book *Dwellers of the Arctic Night*. He went on to explain that this accounts for the phases of the moon. That point was considered by John MacDonald of the Nunavut Research Institute, writing in *The Arctic Sky: Inuit Astronomy, Star Lore, and Legend*. In the everyday lives of the Inuit, the moon was more important than the sun because the solar body "disappeared" for half a year, whereas the lunar body was visible in its various phases throughout the entire year.

Bungees

You have probably heard of bungee jumping: Leaping into space tethered by elastic leashes and bouncing up and down on the rebound. But, did you know that Bungee speaking is (or was) speaking the Chinook Jargon of the West Coast, the lingua franca of the Red River area of Manitoba in the 19th century?

What are the five basic functions of humanity according to the Ojibway?

Native elder Basil Johnston, writing in *The Manitous: The Spiritual World of the Ojibway*, explains that there are five basic functions of humankind. These are leading, defending, providing, healing, and teaching. Each function is represented by its totem, or symbol of a bird, mammal, fish, or fabulous creature that served as a family's emblem. Johnston also explains the meaning of the word *totem:* "The word comes from [the Ojibway word] *dodaem,* meaning action, heart, and nourishment."

What is the meaning of the word "manitou"?

In Ojibway, the language of the Anishinabek Nation, the word *manitou* means mystery, essence, spirit.

The prefix *kitchi* means "grand" in the abstract sense, whereas *mishi* means "grand" in the concrete sense. So one meaning of *kitchi-manitou* is "great (benevolent) spirit," whereas that of *mishi-manitou* is "giant (malevolent) spirit."

Kitchi-manitou, good; *mishi-manitou,* bad.

What is the Aboriginal meaning of the word "Canada"?

The earliest use of the word *canada* was recorded by navigator Jacques Cartier in the account he kept of his voyage up the St. Lawrence River between Quebec and Trois-Rivières in 1535. The place name (or description) of the coast he saw from the deck of his vessel may be derived from the Iroquoian word *kanatas,* meaning "village" or "community."

What is the Aboriginal population?

The country's Aboriginal population in the 2001 census was 975,000, comprising Indians, Métis, and Inuit. The Indians, or members of the First Nations, belong to 11 language groups and collectively speak 50 languages, 12 of which are threatened with extinction. The Inuit traditionally speak dialects of Inuktitut. In the past, the Métis spoke a mixture of French and Cree, what was sometimes called Michif.

What are the three Fs of early Canadian history?

It has been said that the three Fs of early Canadian history are fish, fur, and forests. Indeed, much of the development of the country turned on the exploitation of the fisheries, the fur trade, and the forestry business. Add to that the fourth F and you have faith (i.e., the Church), another driving force for the exploration, occupation, and cultivation of the land and its peoples.

Momentous dates

Here are 10 key dates in Canadian history. Match the dates with the events listed below.

1.	2 May 1670	a.	Battle of the Plains of Abraham
2.	13 September 1759	b.	Confederation of British North America
3.	1 July 1867	c.	Defection of Igor Gouzenko, in Ottawa
4.	16 November 1885	d.	The First World War Armistice: Remembrance Day
5.	11 November 1918	e.	Hudson's Bay Company chartered
6.	15 May 1919	f.	Louis Riel hanged for treason
7.	5 September 1945	g.	October Crisis: FLQ kidnaps James Cross
8.	5 October 1970	h.	Patriation of the Constitution
9.	17 April 1982	i.	Signing of the Free Trade Agreement
10.	2 January 1988	j.	Winnipeg General Strike called

ANSWERS:
1. e; 2. a; 3. b; 4. f; 5. d; 6. j; 7. c; 8. g; 9. h; 10. i.

Dates of disasters

If natural and human history have lessons to impart to us, it is that disasters are always lurking straight ahead or right around the corner. The dates listed below are those of calamities in our country's past. With each date there is a brief description. What happened on each date?

1. 5 February 1663. It took place on land.
2. 29 April 1903. It involved land.
3. 29 May 1914. It took place on water.
4. 3 February 1916. It involved one of the elements.
5. 6 December 1917. It took place in a port city.
6. 19 May 1950. It involved one of the elements.
7. 15 October 1954. It involved one of the elements.
8. 13 October 1958. It took place underground.

ANSWERS:
1. Great Quebec earthquake; 2. The Frank Slide, Alberta; 3. *Empress of Ireland* sinks in the Gulf of St. Lawrence; 4. Fire guts the Centre Block, Parliament Buildings, Ottawa; 5. Halifax explosion; 6. Winnipeg flood, lasting four weeks, at its height on 19 May; 7. Hurricane Hazel, Toronto; 8. Springhill mining disaster, Nova Scotia.

Political catchphrases

Quite often, the tenor of the times is captured in a political catchphrase. It may be a word or a phrase, a bon mot, an aside, or an expression of concern. The phrase may be the work of a single person, or it may be the effort of a group of people. Here are some federal political catchphrases of the 19th and 20th centuries. Complete them. How many of them do you recognize?

1. Reformers in Upper Canada in 1829, desirous of an elected executive, cried for "responsible _____."

2. In his famous report of 1839, Lord Durham found the French and the English to be like "two _____" within a single state.

3. George Brown and others in 1851 called for a recognition of the shift in population when they used the phrase "Rep by _____."

4. Sir John A. Macdonald advocated protectionist measures in 1878 when he announced his National _____.

5. "Laurier and the Larger _____" was the campaign slogan of the Laurier Liberals in 1904.

6. The slogan of the B.C. relief-camp workers of 1938 was "On to _____."

7. In the federal election of 1935, W.L. Mackenzie King tried to convince the electorate the choice was clear: "It's King or _____."

8. The nation was electrified when John G. Diefenbaker campaigned in 1958 and spoke of his _____ vision.

9. Réal Caouette lured the electorate in French Canada into voting for his Ralliement des Créditistes party by asking, "What have you got to _____?"

10. "_____ *chez nous*" was the slogan coined by René Lévesque in 1962 to express the aspirations of the Liberal government in Quebec.

11. Jean Lesage's Liberals attempted, between 1960 and 1966, to bring about a Quiet _____ in Quebec.

12. "_____ Canada" was John G. Diefenbaker's conception of the country in 1962, and it was at variance with Lord Durham's 1839 observation.

13. When elected, Lester B. Pearson promised the nation that his administration would deliver "sixty days of _____."

14. Pierre Elliott Trudeau led the Liberals in their return to power in 1968 with the slogan "The _____ Society."

15. In 1972, NDP leader David Lewis excoriated large corporations, which he characterized as "corporate welfare _____."

16. "_____ association" is a phrase associated in the late 1970s with Quebec premier and Parti Québécois leader René Lévesque.

17. Joe Clark is remembered for his championing of regionalism in 1979 and articulating his vision of Canada as a "community of _____."

18. Prime Minister Brian Mulroney, referring to the Meech Lake Accord in an 11 June 1990 interview, boasted, "It's like an election campaign; you count backward. I said, 'That's the day we're going to _____ _____ _____.'"

19. "I'm the little guy from _____," the then prime minister Jean Chrétien used to boast, thereby misleading the press, which continued to underestimate his talents and tenacity.

20. "His faltering leadership has earned him the sobriquet of ____ _____." That was how the editors of *The Economist* described Prime Minister Paul Martin Jr. on 17 February 2005.

21. Prime Minister Stephen Harper rose in the House of Commons on 22 November 2006 and announced that his government was proposing the motion "that this House recognize that the Québécois _____ ____ _____ within a united Canada."

ANSWERS:
1. government; 2. nations; 3. pop (representation by population); 4. Policy; 5. Canada; 6. Ottawa; 7. chaos; 8. northern; 9. lose; 10. *Maîtres* (Masters in our own house); 11. Revolution; 12. One; 13. decision; 14. Just; 15. bums; 16. Sovereignty; 17. communities; 18. roll the dice; 19. Shawinigan; 20. Mr. Dithers; 21. form a nation.

What lies between Gold and Sword?

The answer is Juno. Gold Beach and Sword Beach flank Juno Beach, the section of the Allied landing coast of Normandy assigned to the Canadian forces. British Infantry divisions stormed Gold and Sword; Canadian infantry divisions took Juno. These divisions consisted of 10 battalions of Canadian infantry supported by three armoured regiments.

Juno is the code name of the amphibious assault on this stretch of the northern coast of Nazi-occupied France, an important part of Operation Overlord, the turning point of the Second World War. It is often described as "the longest day." Ted Barris's *Juno: Canadians at D-Day, June 6, 1944* is a fine account of the Canadian participation in Operation Overlord.

About Juno, Barris wrote: "One amusing story about the coding origins for the Normandy landing sites suggests that SHAEF contemplated naming the British and Canadian beaches after fish; that is, Gold Beach as in goldfish, Sword Beach as in swordfish, and Jelly as in jellyfish. A Canadian, the story continues, informed the British that jelly had a much different and less attractive connotation in North America. Consequently they chose Juno instead."

Some fifteen thousand Canadians participated in the assault on the Juno section of Hitler's "Atlantic Wall." The dead and badly wounded numbered 960. The total invasion force was close to 200,000 men, against an estimated 175,000 German troops who had the benefit of entrenched positions for years. Hitler's vaunted "wall" was breached within hours. The next morning, "D+1," it was apparent that the invading Canadian forces had taken and held more ground than the other Allied forces.

Who was the last Canadian combatant killed during the Second World War, and where is his memorial?

The last Canadian combatant killed during the Second World War was Lieutenant Robert Hampton Gray, a Royal Canadian Navy volunteer reserve pilot and a native of Nelson, British Columbia. He was posthumously awarded the Victoria Cross for bravery. He was 27 years old when he died.

Gray died early on the morning of 9 August 1945, the day an atomic bomb was exploded over Nagasaki. Flying a Corsair launched from the deck of a British aircraft carrier, he was able to sink an enemy warship, but his Corsair, caught in enemy fire, was crippled and he crashed into Onagawa Bay. A memorial to his bravery was erected on 9 August 1989 at Sakiyami Park, which overlooks Onagawa Bay on the coast of Japan's Honshu Island. The memorial was the first on Japanese soil to honour a foreign serviceperson.

Did the Cold War begin and end in Canada?

It is one of the ironies of history that the Cold War, in effect, began and ended in Canada. The Cold War refers to that period of hostilities between the East and the West that lasted from the end of the Second World War to the collapse of Communism and the dissolution of the Soviet Union. Moscow and Washington were at loggerheads, and the rest of the world was imperilled.

It is convenient to date the commencement of hostilities to the defection of Russian cipher clerk Igor Gouzenko from the Soviet Embassy in Ottawa on 5 September 1945. Many months would pass before the public learned the extent of Soviet espionage activities in Canada, the United States, Britain, and other Western countries. A half-century of tension followed.

Less known is the fact that the seeds that ended the Cold War were planted in a field on a farm outside Windsor, Ontario. The farm was that of Eugene Whelan, the folksy minister of agriculture in the Trudeau government. In light of subsequent events, Whelan's signal accomplishment was hosting Mikhail Gorbachev, then the youngest member of the Soviet politburo while on his first tour of a Western country, ostensibly to study agricultural policies and practices for 10 days. The tour took place in May and June 1983, with Gorbachev arriving in Ottawa on 16 May and spending three days there. "In retrospect," wrote Christopher Shulgan in "The Walk That Changed the World," *Saturday Night,* April 2003, "Gorbachev's 1983 tour of Canada was far more important than anyone could have realized."

As accident would have it, the visit to Whelan's farmhouse in the third week of May offered Gorbachev the opportunity to converse unrestrictedly with Alexander Yakovlev, the Soviet ambassador to Canada. Years earlier, Yakovlev had fallen out of favour as the Soviet Union's chief of propaganda and in 1973 was exiled to the Soviet Embassy in Ottawa. He chafed to return to political life in Moscow but, impressed with living conditions in the West, he nurtured plans for badly needed reforms in his homeland, plans he shared with Gorbachev. According to Shulgan, the two men forged their friendship while strolling the grounds of the Whelan farm, with their professional relationship maturing into a personal one. "In a CBC TV documentary," wrote Shulgan, "Yakovlev estimated that 80 percent of the ideas that he discussed with Gorbachev in Whelan's backyard were implemented in perestroika."

Gorbachev returned to Moscow, served under the short-lived administrations of presidents Andropov and Chernenko, and himself served as the 17th and last leader of the Soviet Union from 1985 to 1991. Yakovlev joined him to become Gorbachev's senior adviser. The Berlin Wall fell in 1989; the Soviet Union collapsed in 1991. Glasnost and perestroika were among the many reforms introduced.

So, in a very real sense, the Cold War broke out in Ottawa in 1945. In a symbolic sense, it ended with ideas exchanged and bonds of friendship formed on that farm outside Windsor, Ontario, in 1983. Canada as a country is often described as cold—references to its climate and perhaps to the personality of its people—but it is not a Cold War country.

Where We Live

Place names

There is a town in the Atlantic provinces named after the English chemist and physicist who in 1798 determined the density of the earth and the density of water. Name the town and the province.

ANSWER:
Cavendish, Prince Edward Island, named after the 18th-century English scientist Henry Cavendish.

What Canadian place names are frequently misspelled?

The names of numerous Canadian places are often confused, garbled, or misspelled. Here, in alphabetical order, appear leading place names and their misspellings:

Edmundston, New Brunswick (Edmonston)
Gaspé, Quebec (Gaspe Bay)
Geraldton, Ontario (Geralton)
Sidney, British Columbia (often confused with Sydney, Nova Scotia)
St. Catharines, Ontario (St. Catherine's, St. Catherines)
St. John's, Newfoundland (often confused with Saint John, New Brunswick)

What is the meaning of the place name "Ottawa"?

It is widely believed that the name "Ottawa" is derived from the Algonquian word for barter or trade. If true, this would be fitting, as politicians in the nation's capital are called upon to barter or trade when it comes to policy and power. However, according to Native elder Basil Johnston, a specialist in the Ojibway language, writing in *The Manitous: The Spiritual World of the Ojibway,* it is likely the name of the capital city derives from the Ojibway word *ottauwuhnshk,* which refers to a river reed used for matting, bedding, and making partitions.

Are there "Canadas" in Mexico?

There are. Las Cañadas is the name of a region of Mexico with deep ravines located within the Lacandon Jungle in the province of Chiapas. It is the centre of the Zapatista Native resistance and reform movement. Its name has nothing to do with the country of Canada. In Spanish, the word *cañadas* means "canyons."

The abbreviation of one province is the surname of a famous architect. Which province? Which architect?

P.E.I. was until recently the official abbreviation of the province of Prince Edward Island. (A few years ago, two-letter abbreviations were recognized by Canada Post, so the island is now referred to as PE.) The three-letter abbreviation recalls the last name of I.M. Pei, the Chinese-born American architect famous for his modernist, large-scale projects. Pei designed the Canadian Imperial Bank of Commerce headquarters, Toronto's Commerce Court.

Where in Canada are you always in Love?

Tricky question. The capital letter suggests that *love* is a place name and not a noun describing an emotion. A place name it is.

Love happens to be the name of a village on the Canadian Pacific Railway line in northeast Saskatchewan. It is believed no other place is so named in North America. As for the name itself, the popular notion is that it was called that after young lovers were found on a siding of the newly laid railway tracks, but it is more likely the site was named after CP conductor Tom Love, who dubbed it Love Siding when he passed through in 1930. It became the Village of Love in 1945.

On Valentine's Day 1993, the postmaster first made use of the postmark, adorning it with the image of a seated teddy bear holding upright a giant heart circled by the words "Canada Post—*Postes Canada*—Love, Saskatchewan." Since then, the postmark has been prized by people from around the world, who mail letters to the postmaster in Love requesting the enclosed envelopes be stamped and franked with the desired postmark. On Valentine's Day, the mail is particularly heavy.

The population of Love, Saskatchewan, in 2005 was listed as 51 inhabitants, as noted by Darren Bernhardt in "51 People Who Are Always Truly in Love," *National Post,* 12 February 2005.

What do the place names "Quebec" and "Detroit" have in common?

What these two place names have in common is their etymology. Both *Quebec* and *Detroit* are names derived from Native words that mean "narrows" or "strait," a reflection of their locations on the St. Lawrence and Detroit rivers.

What do Lloydminster and Flin Flon have in common?

Both Lloydminster and Flin Flon are border cities in that they sprawl across provincial boundaries. Lloydminster is mainly in Saskatchewan but partly in Alberta. Flin Flon is in Manitoba, but part of it is also in Saskatchewan.

Why is Canada Day a moving experience in Quebec?

The anniversary of Confederation is celebrated every year on 1 July. It is Canada's national day and Quebec's *le jour sacré de déménagement,* or day dedicated to moving—by tradition, it is the day on which residents move from one residence to another. Leases lapse and take force on 1 July. In 2005, for instance, it was estimated that in Montreal alone some eight hundred families moved on or around 1 July, one-third of that year's moves.

Where is the signpost capital of Canada?

The so-called signpost capital of Canada is Watson Lake in the Yukon Territory. Its motto is "Yukon's Gateway." Visitors to this tiny community with a declining population (approximately fifteen hundred people in 2006) are surprised to discover within the town limits a veritable signpost forest, the signs exhibiting place names, personal names, distances, and directions. "There are at least a couple of dozen for every man, woman and child who lives here," noted writer Mark Richardson in "The Yukon," *The Toronto Star,* 16 March 2006.

The tradition that a visitor erect a signpost dates from 1942 when, it is said, a homesick GI who was working on the Alaska Highway erected his own signpost giving the general direction and the distance in miles to his hometown in the United States. It is said that subsequent visitors have gifted the community with fifty thousand signposts, making it the signpost capital of Canada and the rest of the world.

It seems Watson Lake gives expression to literary critic Northrop Frye's question "Where is here?"

Is Montreal the second-largest, French-speaking city in the world?

It used to be said that Montreal was the world's second-largest, French-speaking city. (Naturally, pride of place went to Paris, as befitting the more populous city and capital of France.) However, during Quebec's Quiet Revolution in the 1960s, followed by that province's passage of French-first, English-second language laws, the claim that Montreal came second went unasserted even in tourist promotion. After all, it was the aim of the Parti Québécois to assert whenever possible that the French language was everywhere endangered, particularly in Quebec. However, Mark Abley, the author of *Spoken Here*, a study of the status of the world's languages, suggests that the silver medal should be awarded to Kinshasa, the much more populous capital of the African country Congo (formerly Zaire). Now that the language known as Congo has replaced French with English as the country's official second language, maybe in the future Montreal, with its current bronze status, will again claim the silver medal.

Did Al Capone go into hiding in Moose Jaw?

Moose Jaw, Saskatchewan, may seem an unlikely place for Al Capone to go into hiding, but the Chicago gangster did disappear for three months in 1926, when U.S. prosecutors tried to indict him for the murder of fellow gangster Joe Howard. No one knows where Al Capone found sanctuary, but local stories are rife with assertions that he took refuge in Moose Jaw.

The city, located on the Canadian Pacific Railway's Soo Line, which runs to Chicago, was easily accessible to Capone. From the early 1920s to the early 1930s, prohibitionists put a damper on the sale of liquor, but gangsters expedited its illegal traffic and trade. It is said that secret tunnels beneath the city's streets were used in the transport of bootleg beverages.

According to reporter Craig Wong, "Canadian Mysteries: Rumours Rife, Hard Evidence Scant on Gangster Al Capone's Time in Moose Jaw," *Ottawa Citizen,* 11 July 2001, local traditions boast of Capone's presence in the city whenever there was "heat" in the Cicero district of Chicago, where he had established his crime empire. Apparently, Capone would take refuge in Moose Jaw's Empress Hotel. To effect quick getaways, he had escape tunnels burrowed beneath the building leading to houses of refuge. Indeed, passageways exist, but these were constructed for maintenance purposes, not for any harried flights by Al Capone.

Natural Assets

How does Canada rank among the world's major fishing countries?

It doesn't. The five largest fishing countries of the world in 2006 were (in decreasing size of industry) Japan, Russia, China, the United States, and Peru. Canada ranked 16th among the world's major fishing countries.

How does Canada rank among the world's top oil producers?

Canada comes in at number 9 among the world's top producers of oil. Saudi Arabia ranks first, followed by Russia, and then the United States. Canada ranks number 15, ahead of the United Arab Emirates.

Which country has the highest expenditures on education?

The answer is surprising. Measured against its gross domestic product (GDP), the country that spends the most money on education is Lesotho, in Africa (approximately 10 percent). Israel comes next (7.3 percent), followed by Portugal (5.9 percent). Canada does not rank among the top 20 countries for educational spending. This is bad news for our students and scholars.

How many of the world's largest banks are Canadian?

In any list of the world's 50 largest banks, not one bank is Canadian. Ten of these banks are based in the United States, five are based in Japan, another five are based in the United Kingdom, and four are in China. The rest of the banks are based in Europe. No Canadian bank is this wealthy.

How many Canadian businesses rank in the world's top 50 largest businesses?

None. The world's five biggest businesses based on sales are (in decreasing order) Wal-Mart, British Petroleum, ExxonMobil, Royal Dutch Shell Group, and General Motors. Canada boasts no companies in the major league. In fact, in a list of 50 of the biggest businesses, not one company is Canadian-owned. The United States has 19, Japan 8, Germany 4, France 4, and the United Kingdom 3. The rest are based in the Netherlands, Italy, and Switzerland.

What is British Columbia's secret resource?

It is generally accepted that the basis of the economy of British Columbia is resource extraction and harvest, notably of oil and gas, and lumber. But that ignores a secret source of its revenue—the province's illicit trade and traffic in marijuana.

In July 2001, the province's Organized Crime Agency estimated that the province has between 15,000 and 25,000 illegal marijuana-growing operations. Each employs six persons and annually produces a crop with a wholesale value of $4 billion. All but 5 percent of the growth is exported to the United States. Export sales of marijuana are estimated to be larger than the export sales of wood and oil and gas, which are legal. It is said that more people are employed growing marijuana than are working in the province's logging, mining, and oil and gas industries combined.

So marijuana cultivation is British Columbia's secret resource. It is also Canada's. Here is what investigative reporter Misha Glenny wrote in "Boom-time for Mafias," in *The Economist's The World in 2007*:

> Thanks to the spread of so-called "grow-ops" (indoor marijuana plantations), Canada is now home to the largest number of criminal syndicates in the world (using, that is, the most common law-enforcement definition that considers three people involved in the commission of a crime to be a syndicate). Marijuana cultivation has allowed crime to break out of the underworld and into the middle-class.

Here is a Canadian first: Canada leads the world in criminal conspiracies!

How does our standard of living compare with Luxembourg's?

Canada's standard of living is only half that of Luxembourg. In fact, the tiny duchy's standard of living is the highest in the world. This is measured in gross domestic product (GDP). Luxembourg also has the world's highest purchasing power. Its GDP is $US52,980, whereas Canada's is number 20 on the list of highest GDP per head at $27,190. As for its purchasing power, Luxembourg's is 147.0 per head (with the United States at 100.0). By this index, Canada ranks number 10, with purchasing power of 79.6. It pays to be a principality rather than a dominion.

Agriculture

It is an interesting agricultural fact that, over the years, the number of family farms in Canada has been decreasing, while the acreage of crops under cultivation and the numbers of livestock have both been increasing. There will be fewer but bigger farms in the future. In 2006, there were some 246,000 farms across the country, with 90 million acres of crops. Included in this figure are the 2230 organic farms, most of which specialize in field crops such as wheat, alfalfa, canola, and barley.

Repasts

Atlantic dishes

What are bannock, brewis, and poutine râpées?

These are dishes served in the Atlantic provinces. Bannock is a Scottish oat cake that is popularly identified as "Indian bread." Brewis is boiled ship's biscuit with codfish (sometimes with potatoes and wild herbs), an English recipe via Newfoundland. Poutine râpées is grated potatoes layered with chicken or beef and is an Acadian dish. They are delicious.

Snack foods

Everyone has his or her favourite snack food. For instance, Pierre Elliott Trudeau enjoyed nibbling on chocolate chip cookies, whereas former Quebec premier Lucien Bouchard always kept a package of Arrowroot biscuits handy for when he was hungry. Former U.S. president Ronald Reagan gobbled jellybeans and George Bush Sr. hated broccoli. The favourite snack food of Prime Minister Stephen Harper is not a matter of public record. Perhaps an investigative reporter (or lifestyle editor) should ask his wife, Laureen.

Where is the potato museum located?

The world's sole museum devoted to the humble potato is the Prince Edward Island Potato Museum. It is found in the town of O'Leary, in the western part of the island. Opened in 1993 and expanded in 1999, the museum opens its doors every summer to visitors and potato-lovers from mid-May to mid-October. Members of the public are greeted by the giant potato, a fibreglass effigy of a potato that rises over 4 metres in height and measures over 2 metres in diameter.

Visitors walk through the Potato History Exhibit, the Machinery Gallery, the Potato Hall of Fame, the Amazing Potato Exhibit, the Community Museum, and the Resource Room (with gift shop), and down Heritage Lane, where they'll find the Heritage Chapel, Log Barn, and Log Railway Station. To be added are a fire hall and telephone office.

The last week in July sees the Potato Blossom Festival. "Bud the Spud" (the phrase is Stompin' Tom Connors') never had it so good. The common potato is an important export of Prince Edward Island. But considering the importance of this vegetable to the health and well-being of humankind (though currently out of fashion with weight-conscious consumers), it is surprising that it has attracted so little research and so little in the way of general interest and appreciation.

What is icewine, and how is it made?

Icewine (spelled as one word) is a premium wine, most if not all of which is produced in the Niagara Peninsula and the Okanagan Valley. "The grapes are left on the vine into early winter, usually until late December or early January. They are picked at night with the temperatures at –8 degrees C so the grapes stay frozen. The temperature is critical because it freezes the water in the grape but not the inner nectar. The grape presses, which are usually moved outside to maintain the cold condition, gently squeeze the grapes as they are brought in from the field. Not much syrup emerges, but it is oh so rich!" So wrote Hans and Allyson Tammemagi in *Exploring Niagara: The Complete Guide to Niagara*

Falls and Vicinity. Icewine, which is expensive to produce, is sold in small, 375-millilitre bottles and makes an excellent dessert wine. Recently, a champagne-like icewine has been made available; it's ideal for toasts.

Whatever is ice cider?

Ice cider is a delicious dessert wine. Its rich taste has been compared to that of crème brûlée. As a food product, it resembles icewine, another Canadian innovation. Ice cider is a wine-like cider, or a cider-like wine.

Ice cider, like traditional cider, is prepared from apples. It takes about 80 apples to produce a half-bottle of ice cider. The juice comes from apples that are harvested in the fall after the first frost. In some instances, apples are picked off the branches while still frozen. The fermentation period is nine months, with the resulting ice cider reaching an alcohol level of about 12 percent. The bottles sell for about half the price of their icewine counterparts.

"Ice cider is poised to take its place alongside maple syrup, tourtière and butter tarts as one of Canada's most popular contributions to the world of gastronomy," wrote Chris Johns in "A Cold Shower for Hot Cider," *Saturday Night,* February 2005.

The notion of using apples rather than grapes to make wine occurred to Christian Barthomeuf, a French vintner who had immigrated to Canada in 1979. He founded his own winery at Hemmingford in Quebec's Eastern Townships in the mid-1990s. Reasoning that apples have a longer growing season than grapes and are less vulnerable to cold weather, he focused on producing a cider-like wine, using McIntoshes (tart) and spartans (sweet). The first ice cider was bottled by Domaine

Pinnacle in 2000. Ice cider from this winery and from other boutique wineries is now available in most Canadian provinces and in many countries. Production takes place in wineries in Quebec, Ontario, Alberta, and British Columbia.

How Canadian is Kraft cheese?

For three-quarters of a century, the name Kraft has identified the leading brand of packaged, processed cheese in North America. J.L. Kraft, who was born in Fort Erie, Ontario, revolutionized cheese production and consumption by inventing "processed cheese." At the age of 29 he moved to Buffalo and then Chicago, where he began supplying cheeses to grocers from a horse-drawn wagon. He founded J.L. Kraft & Bros. Company in 1909 and five years later opened his first cheese factory. In 1916, he patented a cheese pasteurizing process to prevent spoilage and allow cheese to be transported over long distances. The taste of his cheddars was mild rather than sharp, thereby effecting a change in taste preference. The Kraft company was a progressive marketer and promoted brand recognition. In 1933, it began sponsoring the Kraft Music Hall and the Kraft Television Theatre, popular weekly programs. So Kraft cheese, along with its popular product Kraft Dinner, introduced in 1937, is a North American product that grew from Canadian roots.

Making It Work

What greeting did Alexander Graham Bell want callers to use?

Alexander Graham Bell, the inventor of the telephone, had a melodious voice and a distinct way of greeting callers on the telephone. He found "Hello" unmelodious and unappealing. Instead, he asked people to use the nautical expression, "Hoy, hoy!" After all, it was his invention.

Did a Canadian invent the personal computer?

The answer to this question is yes—if any single person is to be credited with the invention of the personal computer. Corporations in the 1960s were using mainframe computers, but the notion that an ordinary person might want to own his or her personal computer for use at home or for a small business was yet to come.

The first personal computer was the MCM/70 microcomputer, with its own built-in microprocessor. In other words, it was not attached to a mainframe. It was designed, built, manufactured, advertised, marketed, and sold to individuals for personal use. It was unveiled in Toronto on 25 September 1973, two years ahead of the debut of the trend-setting Apple 1 PC.

The MCM/70 was pretty primitive in comparison with its successors. It boasted 8 kilobytes of random access memory and 14 kilobytes of read-only memory, and used a tape cassette to save its digits. It was designed and produced by Mers Kutt, a computer specialist, to replace the punch cards that were still being used at Queen's University in Kingston, Ontario, where Kutt was employed at the time. He then formed his own company, Micro Computer Machines Inc., to manufacture and market it.

"The MCM/70 could be described as the Avro Arrow of computing history. It was truly ahead of its time and showed lots of promise, but never quite took off because, at least in part, it was made in Canada—far from computing's heartland," writes Rachel Ross in "Remembering the MCM/70," *The Toronto Star,* 25 September 2003. The MCM/70's pre-eminent position in the world of personal computing is recognized by the journal *IEEE Annals of the History of Computing.*

Did a Canadian invent the flight recorder?

It was not the flight recorder—the black box that records which instruments malfunctioned on a plane that has crashed—that was invented by a Canadian but the crash position indicator, or CPI. Both inventions have proved to be important in civil and military aviation.

The Alberta-born electrical engineer Harry Stevinson—who was associated with the National Research Council—developed a mobile radio beacon that rides near the tail of an aircraft. The beacon takes the form of a "tumbling aerofoil" that weighs only five kilograms. It is a tiny radio transmitter with its own battery, micro-circuitry, and antenna. Its spring-loaded release mechanism is activated upon impact, broadcasting the location of the downed craft. Because it is wrapped in foam plastic, it even floats in water.

Stevinson produced the first working model in the 1960s, and Leigh Instruments manufactured it.

What did Louise Poirier devise?

Louise Poirier designed and named the world's first push-up brassiere with underwire and light padding—known in the undergarment trade as "plunge and push"—to maximize cleavage and minimize the effects of gravity. The name she chose was Wonderbra. At the time—1964—she was working for Canadelle, in Montreal. It was an immediate international success.

Who invented Dick Tracy's wrist radio?

Did a Canadian invent the wrist radio?

Nostalgia buffs know that the wrist radio was the invention of cartoonist Chester Gould. It was worn by Gould's crime-fighting detective Dick Tracy in the inventive Dick Tracy comic strip wildly popular in the late 1940s and early 1950s. But it seems that the wrist radio—along with the original walkie-talkie, and the primitive pager (ideal for medical personnel)—were all the inventions of an engineer named Al Gross. Born in Toronto and raised in Cleveland, Ohio, Gross graduated in electrical engineering from Case School of Applied Sciences (today part of Case Western Reserve University). For the U.S. military's Office of Strategic Services, he developed the ground-to-air, battery-operated radio that could transmit and receive from up to 50 kilometres.

Gross developed the first pager in 1949 and, two years later, the first cell phone. In 1959, he worked on timing devices for Titan, Atlas, and Minuteman missiles. According to the Associated Press obituary, *The Globe and Mail,* 16 January 2001, "His contribution to pop culture came in the late 1940s when Dick Tracy cartoonist Chester Gould visited the Gross workshop. Mr. Gould saw two items that sparked a brainstorm: a watch with a built-in beeper and a wireless microphone. 'Can I use this?' he asked the inventor, who agreed to the request." So in 1949, the comic strip detective made his debut as a crime fighter aided by a two-way wrist radio. Unknown or at least unrecognized by historians of invention in his native Canada, Al Gross at the age of 82 died in Sun City, Arizona, on 21 December 2000.

Many a youngster who read comic books—as this author did—yearned to own a wrist radio. Today it exists, of course, as a wrist telephone and television—in the form of the cell phone with text-delivery system known as the BlackBerry. The BlackBerry was introduced as recently as 1999 by an inventive company called Research in Motion, founded in 1984 in Waterloo, Ontario, and headed by Turkish-born philanthropist Mike Lazaridis.

Is Java a Canadian invention?

Java is not a Canadian invention but it was devised by a former Canadian. James Gosling (born in Calgary, Alberta, in 1956) was the leader of SUN Microsystems's "Green Team," which formed in 1991 and developed the internet programming language known as Java. The original name of the language was First Person, and its original applications were primarily for video. It was later renamed Java—*java* being a colloquial word for coffee. With the mushrooming of the internet, the language was adapted to that use and is now considered the most portable of all programming languages. Gosling once said, "As the world speaks English, Internet speaks Java."

Who learned he was a Nobel Prize laureate while sitting alone on a Moscow Express train that was late leaving the Leningrad Railway Station?

The chemist Gerhard Herzberg was sitting alone in his compartment on the Leningrad–Moscow express train when he was approached by a distinguished-looking gentleman who removed his fur hat, stood at attention, and announced breathlessly, "Professor Herzberg, I am the secretary of the Soviet Academy of Science, and I have the honour to report that you have been awarded the Nobel Prize in physics." The secretary had delayed the train's departure so he could deliver the welcome news.

This incident is described by physicist Boris Stoicheff in his 2002 biography *Gerhard Herzberg: An Illustrious Life in Science.* As he explains it, the German-born Canadian chemist with the National Research Council of Canada was travelling alone at the time, in 1971. His fellow passengers spoke only Russian. Herzberg could only smile to himself for six hours. Amazingly, his first thought was not "Why me?" but "Why physics? Why not chemistry?"

Herzberg was a world authority on molecular structures, founder of the NRC's spectroscopy laboratory in Ottawa, and the author of the classic trilogy of *Molecular Spectra and Molecular Structure, Atomic Spectra,* and *Atomic Structure,* which have influenced generations of scientists.

Is eBay a Canadian success story?

Yes and no. eBay is the name of the leading internet trading service. It has been called "the pioneer of the person-to-person online auction"; since its inception, it has been *the* website to visit to bid on products and services.

The service was founded in 1995 by Pierre Omidyar. Its first employee and first president (regarded as co-founder) is Jeff Skoll, who was born in Montreal in 1965, raised in Toronto, and is a graduate in electrical engineering from the University of Toronto, and an MBA from the Stanford Graduate School of Business. In 2003, *Fortune* magazine listed Skoll as the fourth richest American under the age of 40 (the third being Pierre Omidyar), with his personal wealth estimated at US$2.63 billion.

A man with a social conscience, Skoll promoted the eBay Foundation, a charitable trust; in 1999 he established the Skoll Foundation, based in California's Silicon Valley, for philanthropy, specifically in support of social entrepreneurs and innovative non-profit organizations working to better communities throughout the world.

Omidyar has no known Canadian connection, but it is interesting that the name of eBay brings to Canadian minds The Bay, the trading name of the great fur-trading enterprise, the Hudson's Bay Company (HBC). Founded in 1670, the HBC was the world's oldest incorporated joint-stock merchandising company until the 1990s, when the corporate enterprise collapsed. At the same time, eBay came into existence. The "Bay" of eBay is not that of the HBC but, rather, a nod to the Bay area of San Francisco, the location of that company's corporate headquarters.

Who originated mobile document destruction?

Credit for originating the first mobile document shredding service goes to Greg Brophy, a Toronto businessman who founded Shred-it, a division of Securit Records Management of Oakville, Ontario. In 1987, it occurred to Brophy that a mobile shredding machine was the ideal solution to the need that businesses and corporations had for confidential document destruction. That year he outfitted a van for this sole purpose. The next year, Brophy established his company in Oakville to serve the Greater Metropolitan Area; it wasn't long before mobile shredding vans parked outside corporations and businesses were a common sight in major cities around the world. Shred-it itself has grown to serve 150,000 customers through 130 branches on five continents.

Where is Canada's brightest spot?

The brightest spot in Canada is not the site that boasts the most sunshine. Instead, it is the arena-sized building on the campus of the University of Saskatchewan, in Saskatoon, that houses the country's immense synchrotron. This is the headquarters of Canadian Light Source (CLS), a research facility that combines the interests of academe, government, and industry. The synchrotron it operates—with its immense "rings"—is a kind of accelerator that is able to generate beams of light that are described as "millions of times brighter than the sun." These beams, a form of radiation, are used to illuminate the molecular structure of matter. The CLS is a national undertaking of immense scientific importance. It employs bright people and hence may be regarded as the brightest spot in Canada.

What is the Perimeter Institute?

Everything about the Perimeter Institute is b-i-g—gigantic, in fact. Its full name is the Perimeter Institute for Theoretical Physics. It was officially opened in Waterloo, Ontario, on 23 October 2000, with a $100 million donation made by Mike Lazaridis, president of Research in Motion, the developer of the BlackBerry, the handheld wireless messaging device now in use around the world. The institute's endowment is augmented with grants from various levels of government.

The purpose of the institute is no less than the study of the nature of the universe, with an international focus on cutting-edge research in foundational theoretical physics. It offers leading physicists from around the world five-year fellowships to study quantum gravity, string theory, quantum information theory, and the foundations of quantum mechanics. It sponsors seminars and conferences and organizes public lectures (one of the first was delivered by Oxford mathematician Sir Roger Penrose). Its physicists (currently nine) have cross-appointments with faculty at the nearby University of Waterloo.

The Perimeter Institute is an independent organization, it is engaged in foundational research (that is, non-directed and basic research), it is resident-based (that is, not dictated by an agenda), it is non-hierarchical in faculty structure, and it is very much concerned with communicating with the public the importance of its research. Indeed, one of its publications quotes the words of physicist and Nobel Prize–winner Niels Bohr: "Anyone who has not been shocked by quantum physics has not understood it."

Three significant dates

1. All railway and telephone service was called to a halt for one minute at 6:25 P.M., Sunday, 4 August 1922. Who had died?

2. The blackest day in Canadian aviation history was Friday, 20 February 1959. What happened that day?

3. The floodlights on the roof of the Empire State Building were dimmed on Monday, 9 August 2004. What was being marked?

ANSWERS:

1. Alexander Graham Bell, pioneer in communications and transportation, died at his summer home at Baddeck, Nova Scotia, 2 August 1922. Two days later, railway and telephone service was halted at the hour of his death, as a gesture of respect.

2. On 20 February 1959, the contract for the supersonic jet interceptor—the CF-105—the famous Avro Arrow—was cancelled, sending Canada's innovative aviation program into a tailspin from which it never recovered.

3. Alberta-born Fay Wray died in New York City on 8 August 2004, and the next evening the floodlights atop the Empire State Building were dimmed to mark the passing of Hollywood's "Scream Queen," who was so memorably taken to the top of the tower—a new building and the world's tallest building—by the giant ape in the original 1933 version of *King Kong*.

Other Canadian discoveries, inventions, and achievements

Here goes ...

F.W. (Casey) Baldwin was the first person in the British Empire to fly in an airplane. Frederick G. Banting isolated insulin. Alexander Graham Bell invented, as well as the telephone, the aileron, the part of an airplane's wing that controls lateral balance. J. Armand Bombardier built the first automobile. Norman Breakey devised the paint roller. Thomas Burnley designed the first railway sleeping car. Thomas Carroll constructed the self-propelled combine harvester. Frederick Creed devised the Creed Telegraph System. G.E. Desbarats developed the earliest half-tone reproductions. Robert Foulis build the first steam foghorn. W.R. Franks perfected the first anti-gravity flying suit. Abraham Gesner produced kerosene. James Guillet undertook degradable plastics research. James Hillier built the electron microscope. Arthur Irwin devised the padded baseball glove. Harold Johns undertook cobalt bomb research. D.W. Lings developed the walkie-talkie. T.J. McBride patented the passenger car's vista-dome. Joseph MacInnis developed the Sub-igloo and the Sub-mersible. John McLennan extracted helium. Steve Pasjack devised the tuck-away beer-carton handle. Tommy Ryan invented five-pin bowling. Charles E. Saunders grew Marquis wheat. Arthur Sicard built the first snow blower. William Stephenson successfully radio-transmitted the first newspaper photographs. W.R. Turnbull built the original variable-pitch propeller. James Miller Williams found the first commercially successful oil well. Thomas L. Willison undertook calcium carbide production. J. Tuzo Wilson developed the theory of plate tectonics to account for continental drift.

How many Canadians have been awarded the Nobel Prize?

The Nobel Prizes are the world's most prestigious series of awards. They have been awarded each year since 1901 on 10 December, the anniversary of the death of munitions manufacturer and philanthropist Alfred Nobel. The awards in the categories of chemistry, medicine, physics, literature, and peace are presented in Stockholm; those in economics (a johnny-come-lately category, established by the Bank of Sweden in 1968) in Oslo, Norway.

An inclusive alphabetical list of those laureates with some connection to Canada appears here, along with their field of specialty and the province in which they studied or worked. These men—no women so far—were born in this country, were naturalized citizens, were educated here, were engaged in significant research here, or were designated to accept awards on behalf of international bodies. There are 29 names in all. No doubt the years will add many, many more.

Sidney Altman, chemistry, Quebec
Frederick Banting, medicine, Ontario
Saul Bellow, literature, Quebec
Bertram Brockhouse, physics, Alberta
Val Fitch, physics, Quebec
Ivar Giaever, physics, Ontario
William Giauque, chemistry, Ontario
Roger Guillemin, medicine, Quebec
Ernest Hemingway, literature, Ontario
Gerhard Herzberg, chemistry, Saskatchewan

Charles Higgins, medicine, Nova Scotia
David Hubel, medicine, Quebec
Har Gobind Khorana, medicine, British Columbia
Walter Kohn, chemistry, Ontario
Rudolph Marcus, chemistry, Quebec
Robert Mundell, economics, British Columbia
James Orbinski, peace (Médicins Sans Frontières), Quebec
Lester B. Pearson, peace, Ontario
John Polanyi, chemistry, Ontario
Sir Joseph Rothblat, peace (Pugwash), Nova Scotia
Ernest Rutherford, chemistry, Quebec
Andrew Schally, medicine, Nova Scotia
Arthur Schawlow, physics, Ontario
Myron Scholes, economics, Ontario
Adelaide Sinclair, peace (UNICEF), Ontario
Michael Smith, chemistry, British Columbia
Henry Taube, chemistry, Saskatchewan
Richard Taylor, physics, Alberta
William Vickrey, economics, British Columbia

It is a shame that the Nobel committees have so far failed to award the economics prize to the Antigonish Movement (which promotes rural cooperatives) and the peace prize to Greenpeace (for environmental work). As for literature, setting aside Quebec-born Saul Bellow (and the dubious inclusion of two-time Toronto resident Ernest Hemingway), no Canadian has yet received the literature award, whereas 12 Scandinavian authors may claim that honour. Perhaps the moral is that some Canadian munitions manufacturer or defence contractor should establish Canada's own international awards.

6

Ottawa and All That

Fathers of Confederation

We speak of the Fathers of Confederation, yet there is no such official designation. Still, Sir John A. Macdonald is regarded as *the* Father of Confederation; he served as the country's first prime minister, from 1867 to 1873. Fathers of Confederation are considered to be those delegates who attended one, two, or three of the conferences held in Charlottetown, Quebec City, and London that led to the passing of the British North America Act, 1867, by the British House of Commons. Here's a question about the Fathers of Confederation that few people can answer. How many were there?

ANSWER:
There were 36 Fathers of Confederation, that is, delegates from eastern and central parts of the future country who helped pass the British North America Act, 1867.

Is there a preamble to the Canadian Constitution?

There is no preamble to the Canadian Constitution of 1982. Then prime minister Pierre Elliott Trudeau did compose one, with the assistance of his advisers, but it inspired no one, and it was formally rejected by the provincial premiers.

The *Toronto Star* commissioned a number of distinguished Canadians to compose their own possible preambles. Among the people asked was Pierre Berton, whose prefatory remarks were particularly apt and even witty. The full text of the preamble appeared in the newspaper on 16 April 1982. It goes like this:

> Whereas, we Canadians are the only people in all the Americas to free ourselves non-violently from our European roots;
>
> And, whereas, we have been prepared to wait two centuries to achieve, bloodlessly, what others have seized in a sudden explosion of arms;
>
> And, whereas, this act of gradualism, maddening to some, is at the heart of the Canadian character;
>
> Therefore, we do announce, proclaim, order and establish an all-Canadian constitution, returned to these shores as a symbol of our non-violent, if somewhat phlegmatic and cautious character,
>
> Together with a Charter of Rights, expressly designed to provide future employment to the multitudinous graduates of our law schools;

And we do this with humility and quiet pride, having, alone among our neighbours (though with some considerable name calling), managed to achieve our special form of democracy with a minimum of spilled blood.

(Reprinted by permission.)

Second prime minister

Sir John A. Macdonald became the first prime minister of Canada in 1867. Who was the country's second prime minister?

ANSWER:
Alexander Mackenzie succeeded Sir John A. Macdonald as the second prime minister of Canada in 1873.

Canadian charter

We speak blithely of the Canadian Charter of Rights and Freedoms, which was enacted in 1982. It has a 17-word preamble. I have yet to meet anyone who is familiar with those words, and for good reason, because they are hardly inspired. They go like this: "Whereas Canada is founded upon principles that recognize the supremacy of God and the rule of law."

Political parties

When a federal election is called, the four main political parties swing into action and come into sharp relief. These are the Bloc Québécois, the Conservative Party of Canada, the Liberal Party of Canada, and the New Democratic Party. These are federal parties, although, curiously, the first is a non-contender outside Quebec and so it is federal in name only. In addition to these four main parties, there are eight other federal political parties. Can you name one or more of them?

ANSWER:
Give yourself a point if you answer, "No, I cannot name the eight non-mainstream federal political parties." Then give yourself one point for each of these parties named: Canadian Action Party, Christian Heritage Party, Communist Party of Canada, Green Party of Canada, Libertarian Party of Canada, Marijuana Party, Marxist-Leninist Party of Canada, Progressive Canadian Party.

Is it possible to be an honorary Canadian citizen?

Yes, the Parliament of Canada may bestow the honour of being a Canadian citizen to a foreign citizen if that person shows exceptional merit. Swedish humanitarian Raoul Wallenberg received this honour (posthumously) in 1985, Nelson Mandela in 2001, and Tenzin Gyatso, the 14th Dalai Lama, in 2006.

The Order of Canada is also empowered to recognize the distinction of foreign men and women. For instance, the Aga Khan, leader of the world's Ismaili Muslims, was inducted as commander in 2006.

Is the title "Right Honourable" a distinction reserved for prime ministers?

In the past, the title "Right Honourable" was a designation reserved for prime ministers and certain senior members of the cabinet. Then prime minister Brian Mulroney arranged in 1992 to extend the designation to include individual men and women ostensibly unconnected with public life to acknowledge their outstanding contributions to Canadian society. Mulroney's idea of an outstanding person worthy of the designation if not the honour was publishing baron Conrad Black. After 1992, Black was properly styled the Right Honourable Conrad Black.

What are the Salmon Arm salute and the Shawinigan handshake?

The "Salmon Arm salute" is a jocular reference to the finger that the then prime minister Pierre Elliott Trudeau gave to hecklers of his election campaign in Salmon Arm, British Columbia, in the summer of 1983.

The "Shawinigan handshake" is another facetious reference, this one to former prime minister Jean Chrétien giving an obstreperous protestor a form of half nelson in Ottawa, on 16 February 1996.

What is remarkable about the portrait of Brian Mulroney in the House of Commons?

By tradition, portraits of retired prime ministers are commissioned by Parliament and then hung in its halls.

Russian-born artist Igor Babailov painted the official portrait of Brian Mulroney. Upon its unveiling on 19 November 2002, commentators noted that there is "an inscrutable look" on the former prime minister's face. The phrase is that of Hugh Winsor in his column "The Power Game" in *The Globe and Mail*, 20 November 2002. "[Babailov] painted Mr. Mulroney with a smile that from some angles turns into a smirk."

The effect is curious and perhaps contrived. Was it calculated, like Louis-Philippe Hébert's life-size statue of Evangeline in Grand-Pré National Park, Nova Scotia, which, depending on the viewer's vantage point, depicts the Acadian heroine as a happy young girl or as a sad older woman?

How We Live

What is the best country in the world in which to live?

There is no answer to this question, but each year the United Nations offers criteria that could help a person make up his or her mind about which country is the best in which to live. It releases the UN Development Index, which is based on an analysis of 177 countries in terms of health, education, life expectancy, income levels, poverty levels, and environment.

Luxembourg has a higher standard of living than does Canada, but living standards may be read in various ways. Canada was at the top of the UN's list between 1992 and 2001. Since then it has been the "undevelopment" list for Canadians—Canada ranks number 6 on the list the UN released on 9 November 2006. Ahead of Canada are (starting at the top of the list) Norway, Iceland, Australia, Ireland, and Sweden. Immediately behind Canada are Japan and the United States. What will it take for

Canadians to regain top honours? Attention must be paid to the indicators: health, education, poverty levels, and environment.

How do we assess the fitness of a country?

Assessing the fitness of a country is a personal matter, but George Faludy, Hungary's leading poet and humanist at the time of his death in 2006, might be considered an expert in such matters, as he spent time in concentration camps under both Fascists and Communists in his native land. Immigrating to Canada in 1967, he acquired citizenship, returning to Hungary after the collapse of Communism, in 1987. Having lived in many countries, including the United States, where he served in the U.S. Army during the Second World War, he became a connoisseur of countries as well as of prisons.

He evolved "ten considerations" by which to measure the quality of life in the countries of the world. These considerations have little to do with ideology and technology, with materialism and idealism, or with the UN Development Index. Instead, they have to do with civility and the human spirit. In the pages of his book *Notes from the Rainforest,* which consists of observations and meditations on man, society, history, and nature, written in a cabin in the Interior of British Columbia, he offers a considered list of considerations:

1. Freedom to leave without an exit visa or baggage search is assumed.
2. Faces of the population are generally cheerful.
3. Public rudeness is rare.

4. Fairly elaborate manners are expected of everyone after the age of seven.
5. Public libraries are uncensored, well-stocked, and much-used.
6. Little or no hunger or squalor is evident, though the accumulation of wealth is not generally thought of as the meaning of life.
7. Violence is rare and, among the police, severely forbidden.
8. A general attitude is live and let live.
9. No political prisoners are taken.
10. Few are destitute and those few are charitably treated.

What to make of this sobering list? Faludy continues: "It will be seen at once that a few countries (Iceland, Denmark, Canada) come off reasonably well, with others (e.g., Tunisia, Costa Rica, France, the United States) hovering somewhere in the middle ground. At the bottom, as on anybody's scale, will be such nightmares as Uganda, Albania, Cambodia, Honduras, etc." (Courtesy of the Dundurn Group.)

Faludy's readers will likely conclude with him that indeed Canada has "come off reasonably well." But it is important to bear in mind that trends in the modern world—fundamentalism of all stripes, unconstrained globalization of work and products and services, consumerism, communications consolidation, and so on—tend to undermine these important considerations.

Which four urbanized regions hold 51 percent of our population?

Canada is a more urbanized country than the United States. Our population is concentrated in cities. Four urbanized regions account for 15.3 million people (51 percent of the population). These regions are Metropolitan Montreal; the Golden Horseshoe of Ontario; the Calgary–Edmonton corridor; the Lower Mainland–South Vancouver Island.

Scattered across the country, sometimes collected in smaller urban centres, are found the remaining 49 percent of the population. So the chances are better than average that you, the reader, live in one of these four heavily populated regions.

Religious affiliations

If there are 10 Canadians in a room, 5 of them are Roman Catholic, and 3 of them are Protestant. The remaining 2 people represent members of other religious groups, e.g., Jewish, Islamic, Sikh. That's a rough breakdown, the percentages being 50 percent and 30 percent, respectively. That totals 80 percent; the remainder (20 percent) accounts for people of other faiths. Over the years, the number of Roman Catholics has been increasing more than that of Protestants, but both increases reflect a downward trend in terms of the total population. The other religious groups are gaining ground.

Same-sex couples

Although it does not keep detailed records of these matters, Statistics Canada reported that in the year 2001 there were 34,200 same-sex common-law couples in the country (0.5 percent of all couples). Most of these couples were male–male, rather than female–female. This finding was made before the court's recognition of the right of gay couples to marry.

Dual citizens

A dual citizen is a person who holds citizenship of two or more countries. Canadian law has recognized dual citizenship since 15 February 1977. For practical purposes, it means that a citizen may legally and simultaneously hold both a Canadian passport and the passport of a foreign country. Statistics Canada reported that there were 553,000 dual citizens in 2001. This means that about 5.5 percent of the Canadian population bear dual citizenship.

The Queen holds Canadian citizenship, as well as 16 other citizenships. The subject of divided allegiances came to public attention in August 2005 when it was noted that the Governor General–designate, Michaëlle Jean, a native of Haiti, was both a citizen of France through marriage and a citizen of Canada through naturalization. Stéphane Dion, elected leader of the Liberal Party of Canada in December 2006, saw no reason to renounce his French citizenship (his mother was born in that country) any more than his Canadian citizenship (he and his father were born in Canada), maintaining it is no conflict of interest.

Immigrants and refugees

Immigration is under scrutiny as never before. In the year 2002, Toronto was the destination of choice for almost half of all immigrants, with Vancouver following at a close second. Together the two cities account for over 60 percent of all immigrants, a total of some 262,000 newcomers in 2006. The same settlement pattern applies to the annual intake of 25,000 refugees.

What is the country's population?

The country's population (in 2004) was estimated at 31,946,316. There are said to be six billion people globally, so Canada's population is a drop in the population bucket.

If you divide the population into the country's total area, you will find that there is close to 0.4 square kilometres for each person in the country. That is a lot of legroom. Yes, it is a *big* country.

How old are we?

Look around you. The median age of a Canadian (in 2003 anyway) was 37.9 years. That is, half the population is older than that age, half the population younger than that age. Older people are congregated in the east—in the four Atlantic provinces—and in Quebec. The youngest people (22.9 years) are found in Nunavut.

Is our population increasing or decreasing?

Where can one turn for an up-to-the-minute estimate of the population of Canada? That's a simple question because all you have to do is type into an internet search engine (e.g., Google) the words "Canada's population clock" to read an estimate of the country's population that very minute. There is no need to wait for the next decennial census (in the year 2011) to know the number of people who live here. In general, the population increases by one birth every 1 minute, 32 seconds; decreases by one death every 2 minutes, 14 seconds; increases through immigration by one person every 2 minutes, 24 seconds. The estimated population for 1 July 2007 is 32,950,394.

Who has the longest life expectancy?

On average, as things stand, men may expect to live 77.0 years, women 82.9 years. Life expectancy is highest in British Columbia of all the provinces and territories. So head west, and live 78.0 years (if you are male) or 82.9 years (if female).

Mortality alas

Despite Canadians' relatively long life expectancy, everyone has to die. Here are the top five causes of death for both men and women: neoplasm (cancer); ischemic heart disease; diabetes mellitus; traffic accident; intentional self-harm.

The military

Personnel

Are you able to name the offices of the two most senior Canadian military personnel?

That question may be answered correctly with either a yes or a no answer.

ANSWERS:
The yes answer goes like this: The two most senior positions are commander-in-chief (the person of the Governor General) and the Chief of the Defence Staff (an appointed military position).

The no answer goes like this: No, I cannot.

Both answers are correct.

Being defensive

Which organization operates CFBs, CFSs, ASUs, CFSUs, FOLs, and WATCs? And what do the initialisms represent?

ANSWERS:
The National Defence Headquarters in Ottawa operates the country's military installations. There are 34 such installations across the land. The initialisms: CFBs (Canadian Forces bases), CFSs (Canadian Forces situations), ASUs (area support units), CFSUs (Canadian Forces support units), FOLs (forward operating locations), and WATCs (Western area training centres).

Whatever is DART?

The Canadian Armed Forces authorized the formation of the Disaster Assistance Response Team in the 1990s. Popularly known as DART, it consists of a team of military personnel, including soldiers, doctors, and engineers, who are specially trained in emergency relief operations. DART's home base is CFB Trenton, Ontario, and its response time is 48 hours. DART has been on standby except for three foreign-disaster relief missions: Honduras hurricane (1998); Turkey earthquake (1999); Sri Lanka (2004–05). The last mission was in response to the undersea earthquake in December 2004 that produced the Asian tsunami and resulted in the deaths of over 100,000 people from the littorals of more than one dozen Asian countries.

What is the C7?

C7 is the designation of the assault rifle that is the standard equipment of the Canadian Armed Forces. Its magazine holds 30 rounds and its rate of fire is 700 to 940 rounds per minute, with a range of 400 metres. It was designed in the mid-1980s for close-quarter battle. Based on the United States's M16, it is the weapon of choice of Britain's Special Air Service (SAS), having outperformed SAS's SA80 and the American M16. The C7 is manufactured by Diemaco of Kitchener, Ontario.

The Mounties

"They always get their man" is *not* and has never been the official motto of the Royal Canadian Mounted Police, despite the best efforts of well-wishers like Hollywood and the Disney Corporation. What *is* the official motto in French and English?

ANSWER:
The RCMP's official motto is *Maintiens le droit* / Uphold the right.

Who is Dudley Do-Right?

Writers Alex Anderson and Jay Ward created the character of Dudley Do-Right, the upright, unbright Mountie, as long ago as 1948. It was not until 1961 that the animated character first appeared as a segment of the TV program *The Bullwinkle Show*. Then Dudley had his own series of brief episodes (each four and a half minutes in duration) on CTV Alberta in 1969–70.

The incompetent Dudley was modelled on Nelson Eddy's Mountie character in the movie *Rose-Marie*. He is supervised by Inspector Fenwick in his battle against his arch enemy, Snideley Whiplash, who repeatedly kidnaps Dudley's girlfriend, Nell, the inspector's daughter, and ties her to railroad tracks. Snideley has green skin. According to Michael Dawson in *The Mountie: From Dime Novel to Disney*, Ward has described Dudley as "stalwart, clean-living, chaste, dense—and a crashing bore."

Edifices of eminence

Seven great architects

Match the architect with the landmark Canadian building.

1. Douglas J. Cardinal	a. Canadian Museum of Civilization, Ottawa
2. Arthur Erickson	b. Château Frontenac, Quebec City
3. I.M. Pei	c. Empress Hotel, Victoria
4. Moshe Safdie	d. Habitat, Montreal
5. Bruce Price	e. Massey College, Toronto
6. F.M. Rattenbury	f. Museum of Anthropology, Vancouver
7. Ron Thom	g. Place Ville Marie, Montreal

ANSWERS:
1. a.; 2. f; 3. g; 4. d; 5. b; 6. c; 7; e.

Are there palaces and castles in Canada?

Our country has no palaces, but it does have castles, or at least imposing residences designed and erected in the English and French manner that is often identified with the traditional castle.

One thinks of Toronto's Casa Loma (built by Sir Henry Pellatt) and Castle Frank (A.E. Kemp); Hamilton's Dundurn Castle (Allan MacNab); Montreal's Glencoe (Lord Strathcona); Victoria's Craigdarroch Castle (Robert Dunsmuir). In addition, Canadian Pacific's mansard-roofed hotels recall the traditional château architecture of France. Although the allegiance of Canadian citizens officially lies with the monarchy, no castles fit for kings and queens were erected on our shores since the Second World War.

Residences of renown

Below are listed seven stately homes of historic interest, followed by the names of their occupants and their locales. Match them up.

1. Château St. Louis

2. Chiefswood

3. Clifton

4. Dundurn

5. Dunsmuir

6. Earnscliffe

7. Ravenscrag

a. Sir Hugh Allan, Montreal, Quebec

b. Samuel de Champlain, Quebec City, Quebec

c. Sir James Dunsmuir, Victoria, British Columbia

d. T.C. Haliburton, Windsor, Nova Scotia

e. Pauline Johnson, Brantford, Ontario

f. Leader of the Opposition's residence, Ottawa, Ontario

g. Sir Allan McNab, Hamilton, Ontario

ANSWERS:
1. b; 2. e; 3. d; 4. g; 5. c; 6. f; 7. a.

Does Toronto's City Hall appear in a Star Trek episode?

Indeed it does. The episode of *Star Trek: The Next Generation* titled *Contagion*, 20 March 1989, shows Captain Picard and Data standing before an Iconian gateway. This is a portal that allows them to travel to various points in the galaxy. "Various locales appear, including the bridge of the *Enterprise* and the unmistakable fountains of Nathan Phillips Square and the uniquely curved towers of Toronto City Hall." This information comes from "Cityscape," *Toronto Post City Magazine*, December 2003.

Health care

Who was the first person to benefit from insulin?

Leonard Thompson was the first person in the world to benefit from the insulin treatment for diabetes. The 13 year old was facing imminent death when Dr. Frederick Banting persuaded the boy's parents to agree to an experimental treatment that might prolong his life. The afternoon of 11 January 1922, at the Toronto General Hospital, the patient was injected with 15 c.c. of the extract devised by Dr. Banting that is now known as insulin. There was a dramatic, immediate, and observable improvement in Leonard's condition, an improvement that was subsequently dubbed "the resurrection effect." Through repeated injections, his health was stabilized. Leonard defied all the odds and was alive and well some 30 years after the experimental treatment.

Who is the sole non-physician commemorated by the Canadian Medical Association?

The sole non-physician to be commemorated by the Canadian Medical Association (CMC) is T.C. (Tommy) Douglas. In October 1998, a dozen years after his death, he was inducted into the CMC's Hall of Fame as the "Father of Medicare." The citation notes: "His leadership has provided long-term benefits to medical science in Canada, and a Canadian health-care system [that is] a source of envy to other countries." The citation fails to mention that in 1962, the CMC attempted to block the implementation of the form of medical insurance introduced by Tommy Douglas, first in Saskatchewan and then across the country. The irony of this was noted by Ed Finn in "The Father of Medicare," *The CCP Monitor,* February 2005. In fall 2004, the CBC's search for "the greatest Canadian" ended with Tommy Douglas's victory, 100 years after his birth, and 18 years after his death.

Most influential concept in medicine

The most influential concept in medicine of the last half-century might well be the notion of evidence-based medicine. EBM, as it is sometimes called, is described as a way of practising and teaching clinical medicine whereby external evidence is explicitly integrated with clinical expertise and patient preferences to improve clinical decision making.

The phrase *evidence-based medicine* was first used by David Guyatt, professor of medicine and clinical epidemiology and biostatistics at McMaster University in Hamilton, Ontario. He coined this important and influential term in the fall of 1990, and since then the initialism "EBM" and the approach are widely used in medical education and clinical practice.

The notion has less appeal to homeopaths and naturopaths, who prefer to regard their pharmacopoeia as experience-based medicine.

Going under

If you have need of a surgical procedure under anaesthesia, mentally give thanks to Dr. Harold Griffith. Dr. Griffith was an anaesthetist at the Homeopathic Hospital in Montreal (now the Queen Elizabeth Hospital) and an early advocate of keeping detailed records on the anaesthesia performed. On 23 January 1942, he and his colleague Dr. Enid Johnson made medical history during an appendectomy operation when he added curare (a dart poison from Latin America) to the anaesthesia to relax the patient's muscles in addition to inducing the controlled coma. As one medical historian wrote, "It would be hard to envisage how open heart, organ transplant, and radical brain and cranio-facial surgery could have developed without muscle relaxants."

Why did the National Museum of Man change its name?

The National Museum of Man was established in Ottawa in 1841 as a geological and natural history museum. The institution changed its name to the Canadian Museum of Civilization in 1987. The name was changed because it was felt that the word *man* was discriminatory of women and not inclusive of both men and women. The institution is in Hull, Quebec, across the river from Parliament Hill.

Is it railroad or railway?

The first is American, the second Canadian. "Attentive readers will have noted that I have been trying to distinguish between 'railroad' and 'railway.' In the United States it is always railroad, in Canada it is railway. Gordon Lightfoot's famous song about the building of the CPR is called 'The Canadian Railroad Trilogy'; it ought to be called 'The Canadian Railway Trilogy.'" So wrote Wayne Grady in his informative book *Chasing the Chinook: On the Trail of Canadian Words and Culture.*

People Coming and Going

Where is Pier 21?

Pier 21 is the port on the Halifax waterfront that received immigrants and refugees arriving by ship from countries in Europe and elsewhere. Between 1928 and 1971, when it was closed, Pier 21 received one million newcomers. During the Second World War, one-half million servicemen and servicewomen left for overseas from Pier 21, so Pier 21, in its way, holds as many memories as does New York's Ellis Island. It is now a National Historic Site; since 1999, it has served as a museum. The Rudolph Peter Bratty Exhibition Hall offers visitors mementoes of the close to half a century when Pier 21 temporarily housed the hopes and allayed the fears of new Canadians. So far, it has attracted more than two million visitors.

Do new Canadians receive free Bibles?

For about 50 years, free copies of the King James version of the Bible were presented to all new Canadians at citizenship ceremonies. The Bibles were donated by the Canadian Bible Society. The practice of such presentations was discontinued in 1998 in the interests of multiculturalism, freedom of religion, and a separation of church and state.

The Bible Society objected. According to Leslie Scrivener, "Welcome to Canada: Bring Your Own Bible," *Toronto Star*, 26 December 2004, its national director argued, "We are very concerned that this is not protecting the rights of Canadians—it's taking away rights. If you exclude something how are you protecting people's freedom? What if most people want them?"

The discontinuation of the practice was supported by the Humanist Association of Canada, which recommended that the oath of allegiance be based on a non-religious statement.

Is there a distinctive Canadian speech?

Our American cousins are forever assuring us that we speak with an accent. When pressed, Americans will instance the way Canadians pronounce the first and third words in the expression "out and about." They think we say "oot and aboot." You explain it.

We feel there are two things distinctive about our speech patterns. We tend to append *eh?* at the end of a sentence, and we pronounce the last letter of the alphabet as *zed* rather than *zee.*

Some Americans use *eh?* in this way, but none of them pronounces the 26th letter of the alphabet to rhyme with *bed.* You explain it.

The Canadian Oxford Dictionary defines *eh* as an informal interjection, one that may "invite assent" or "ascertain comprehension." "This is the only usage of *eh* that can be categorized as peculiarly Canadian," the editors explain, "all other uses being common amongst speakers in other Commonwealth countries and to a lesser extent in the United States." Other uses include expressing surprise and asking for a repetition or an explanation.

The British and Canadian pronunciation of the letter *z* is *zed* and is derived through the French word *zède* from the Greek word *zeta.*

Symbolic women

Are there women who are symbolic of Canada? Yes and no.

France has its Marianne; the United States its Statue of Liberty. England has its John Bull, but no female icon. Canada has boasted two male figures—Johnny Canuck and the Mountie—but no representative women. Yet, there are some female figures, both imaginary and real, that are so popular they might be said to represent aspects or parts of the country.

"The Spirit of Canada" is the name given the statue of the draped, mourning woman that stands on the dais of the Canadian National Vimy Memorial in France. It was sculpted by Walter Allward to represent grieving motherhood.

Evangeline, the victim of the forced evacuation of the Acadians from their land and the heroine of Wordsworth's narrative poem, is especially honoured in the province of New Brunswick.

Laura Secord, the heroine of the War of 1812, is regarded as a grim, determined, Loyalist housewife who helped thwart the Yankee invasion of the Niagara Peninsula.

Anne Shirley, the heroine of *Anne of Green Gables,* is certainly regarded as the epitome of innocence and virtue, pluck and the spirit of adventure throughout the province of Prince Edward Island and, indeed, around the world wherever L.M. Montgomery's novels are read.

St. Anne, the mother of the Blessed Virgin Mary, is held in high esteem—as is the Virgin Mary herself—in the province of Quebec. Indeed, Roman Catholics honour St. Anne as the patron saint of Canada.

Susannah Sheldon is the high-spirited, fictional heroine of a series of novels, beginning with the *Susannah of the Mounties,* written by Muriel Denison. She is a little Miss Fix-it at Mountie headquarters in Regina. Shirley Temple played the lead in the 1936 movie of the same name about the little girl who teaches officer Randolph Scott how to tap dance and boosts the morale of the force.

N.B. There are many real-life women who have shown indomitable spirit despite the vicissitudes of life and hence are worthy of being regarded as heroines. The list certainly includes artist and essayist Emily Carr, who is greatly admired for her images of nature and Native life.

Who is the Canadian who almost climbed Mount Everest?

History speaks highly of achievers; it should also speak of those who failed by a hair's breadth to achieve life's goals through no fault of their own. Earl C. Denman, a Canadian-born, South African mountaineer, made an unofficial, unauthorized assault on Mount Everest with Tenzing Norgay, the Sherpa who later accompanied mountaineer Sir Edmund Hillary on his successful assault five years later. In his 1954 memoir *Alone to Everest,* Denman described the ordeal in 1947 that almost ended in his death.

Did a drug smuggler advertise for work in a daily newspaper?

As surprising as it might seem, a former marijuana smuggler, who had served time in prison for his offence, did place an advertisement for work in a daily newspaper.

The following is part of what appeared on the Classifieds page of the *National Post's Financial Post,* 19 February 2001: "Former Marijuana Smuggler / Having successfully completed a ten year sentence, incident-free, for importing 75 tons of marijuana into the United States, I am now seeking a legal and legitimate means to support myself and my family."

It was a long advertisement and an interesting one, so it generated media interest and, more important, employer interest. He landed a position.

The newspaper, sensing a story of human interest, interviewed the originator of the paid advertisement in a front-page story titled "'I Can Do Anything an MBA Can.'" Journalist Charlie Gillis identified the former international drug smuggler as Brian O'Dea, who was born in Newfoundland, worked in the United States, and wanted to become a Toronto-based businessman (which he did).

The *National Post* ran the advertisement for six consecutive days, whereas *The Globe and Mail* had declined to print it at all. In a follow-up story carried the next day, "Former Smuggler Secures Job Offers," Gillis noted that O'Dea received "50 media calls and a few firm job offers on the first day that his frank advertisement ran on this newspaper's classified pages." Such is the power of the press and the belief that a person, sufficiently motivated, may change his or her ways.

Who was Canada's first woman mayor?

The temptation is to answer this question by replying that Charlotte Whitton was the first woman to be elected mayor of a Canadian city. That is true, for Ms. Whitton was the first woman to serve as mayor of the city of Ottawa. A former social worker, she served with distinction as a controller and then, upon the death of the incumbent in 1951, as mayor. The following year, she was elected mayor. In the process she gave a leg-up to women in public life.

The key word here is not *first* or *woman* but *city*.

It is equally true that the first woman to be elected the mayor of any municipality in Canada was Barbara Hanley. On 6 January 1936 she was elected by the residents of Webbwood, a town some 80 kilometres west of Sudbury, Ontario. A schoolteacher by profession, Mrs. Hanley served for 12 years on the public school board and then one year on the town council. She retired as mayor after eight consecutive terms. Thereupon she was appointed clerk-treasurer of Webbwood. She died in 1959 at the age of 76, the first woman to be elected mayor in any municipality in Canada.

For this information I am indebted to Mrs. Grace LeBlanc, of Guelph, Ontario, who felt that Mrs. Hanley should receive her due. And I agree.

Quote quiz

Match the famous Canadian quotation with the person who first uttered it.

1. The medium is the message.

2. Goods Satisfactory or Money Refunded.

3. The 20th century belongs to Canada.

4. Fuddle duddle.

5. Literature is conscious mythology.

6. I am a great believer in luck, and I find the harder I work the more I have of it.

7. There are strange things done in the midnight sun / By the men who moil for gold.

8. The grim fact is that we prepare for war like precocious giants and for peace like retarded pygmies.

9. Dreams are made if people try.

10. He shoots! He scores!

a. Timothy Eaton

b. Terry Fox

c. Northrop Frye

d. Foster Hewitt

e. Sir Wilfrid Laurier

f. Stephen Leacock

g. Marshall McLuhan

h. Lester B. Pearson

i. Robert W. Service

j. Pierre Elliott Trudeau

ANSWERS:
1. g; 2. a; 3. e; 4. j; 5. c; 6. f; 7. i; 8. h; 9 b; 10. d.

Who was the so-called Prisoner of Ottawa?

Otto Strasser answered to the depiction of himself as the Prisoner of Ottawa. Strasser was a German ideologue and member of the Nazi Party who struggled with Adolf Hitler over the direction the party should take. Hitler won control and took the party to the right rather than to the left; Strasser was exiled first from the party and then from Germany, in 1933. The Gestapo and the SS trailed him across Europe, and he was lucky to find refuge in Canada in 1941, settling first in Montreal and then in the towns of Clarence and Paradise, Nova Scotia, where he lived with families of sympathizers.

In 1945, he appealed for the right to return to Germany, but he was denied travel documents and forbidden to propagandize for a fascist government in Germany by a joint agreement among the Allied powers, the Canadian government, and the new West German government. Following petitions, appeals, and threatened lawsuits, he was finally able to return to his homeland in 1955. He died in Munich in 1974, outliving the Nazi dictator by almost three decades and becoming an icon of neo-Nazism. Although he was partly responsible for the formation of the Nazi Party, he spent the war years abroad and never engaged in acts of sabotage. Indeed, he was among the first to protest against Hitlerism.

During the 14 years he spent in exile in Quebec and Nova Scotia, he contributed articles to foreign publications. He refined his radical leftist views, which included the need for the authoritarian state, nationalization of industry and industrial property, land distribution to labourers, and anti-Semitism in theory and practice. His theory of revolutionary nationalism—as distinct from the Communist notion of proletarian internationalism—contributed to the revival of neo-Nazi ideologies from the 1960s to the present day. Hitler regarded Strasser as an "intellectual crank"; the Allied governments saw him as an unpredictable element in postwar Europe—an incorrigible thug and a "hot potato."

Dying words

Former prime minister Mackenzie King's dying words, spoken to his nurse in the hospital, were "Thank you."

Famous humorist Stephen Leacock's last recorded words, also spoken to his nurse in the hospital, were "I was a good boy, wasn't I?"

People we love to hate

Adrien Arcand, a leading Fascist in the 1920s and 1930s, was anti-Communist and anti-Semitic, as well as pro-Catholic and pro-Quebec. R.B. Bennett, who was unlucky enough to serve as prime minister during the worst years of the Great Depression, offered no relief measures and, of equal importance, no hope to unemployed men and women. Paul Bernardo with his then girlfriend Karla Homolka was responsible for the horrible deaths of the latter's younger sister and two teenage girls in St. Catharines, Ontario. François Bigot, the corrupt intendant of New France, was responsible for undermining the French forces under Marquis de Montcalm before the battle on the Plains of Abraham. Sir Joseph Flavelle, meat-packing magnate and financier, was accused of profiteering in the sale of foodstuffs to the troops overseas during the First World War. Charles Lawrence, Lieutenant-Governor of Nova Scotia, ordered the deportation of the Acadians in 1755, thereby earning the undying enmity of those French-speaking people to this day. Kurt Meyer was a corporal of the Hitler Youth 12th SS Panzer Division who ordered the murder of 11 captured Canadian soldiers at l'Abbaye de Ardenne near Caen on 7 June 1944. Clifford Olson brutally murdered at least 11 youngsters in British Columbia and was paid for his detailed confession by the RCMP. Robert William Pickton is accused of murdering 27 women and disposing of their bodies on his pig farm in Port Coquitlam, British Columbia. Fred Rose, the only Communist to sit in the House of Commons, was fingered by Igor Gouzenko as a Soviet spy. Paul Rose was a leading member of the FLQ, which took credit for kidnapping

James Cross and murdering Pierre Laporte at the height of the October Crisis of 1970. Robert Stobo, a Scots-born Virginian with the French army, it is said, acted as a turncoat and revealed to General Wolfe and his troops the route to take to scale the cliffs to reach the Plains of Abraham.

People we love

Norman Bethune organized the world's first mobile blood-transfusion service. Cyrus Eaton sponsored the original Pugwash Conference on Science and World Affairs at the height of the Cold War in 1957 whereby scientists from the Soviet bloc were able to meet with their Western counterparts to ease concern over the atomic threat. Jean Vanier gave hope to the world's handicapped men and women when he founded, in 1964, the L'Arche community for men and women with developmental difficulties. M.M. Coady, priest and adult educator, headed the Antigonish Movement, which introduced co-op principles to the fisherfolk of the Maritimes and then to the underdeveloped regions of the world. Tommy Douglas's drive and determination established medicare in his native province of Saskatchewan and then across Canada. Terry Fox, more than a one-legged runner, became an inspiration to millions of people who continue his Marathon of Hope for relief from cancer. Chief Dan George, a former longshoreman, became an eloquent spokesman for the Native peoples of Canada. Josiah Henson, an escaped slave, so loved freedom that his life (and log cabin near Chatham, Ontario) inspired the abolitionist novel *Uncle Tom's Cabin*. A.R. Kaufman, an industrialist and philanthropist, ensured that information on family planning was made legally available to all. Henry Morgentaler changed Canadian law by providing safe abortion procedures as part of overall medical care. Sir William Osler, physician and teacher, introduced the "beside manner" into hospitals in Canada, the United States, and Great Britain. Wilder Penfield, neurologist and surgeon at the Montreal Neurological Institute, mapped the functions of the human brain and was known in the middle of the last century as "the greatest living Canadian."

Games We Play

Where is North America's oldest annual sporting event held?

North America's oldest annual sporting event is held in St. John's, Newfoundland. The inaugural race of the St. John's Regatta was held in the city's harbour on 22 September 1818, to celebrate the 58th anniversary of the coronation of King George VIII. A decade later, the contest moved to Quidi Vidi Lake, in the city's east end, where it has been held annually ever since. The racing event draws four hundred competitors—two-thirds of them female, according to John DeMont, "Homage to Tradition," *Maclean's,* 4 August 2003.

What are Babe Ruth's Canadian connections?

The American baseball star hit his first home run in a minor league game at Toronto's Hanlan's Point Stadium on 5 September 1914. Legend has it the ball disappeared into Lake Ontario, an incident described in Jerry Amernic's delightful novel *Gift of the Bambino*. A municipal marker identifies the site. According to urban legend, the baseball Ruth hit splashed into the waters of Lake Ontario and has subsequently been retrieved and preserved as a souvenir.

As baseball historian William Humber, writing in "The Canada Connection," *Maclean's,* 2 September 2002, notes, "Ruth's life is a veritable treasure house of Canadiana." He was taught to play baseball by a Xaverian Brother named Matthias, born in Lingan, Nova Scotia. His first wife was Helen Woodford from Halifax. A Quebec City–born Red Sox owner brought him to Boston. His longest home run was 183 metres at Montreal's Guybourg Ground in an exhibition game in 1926.

Humber has many more tidbits in his column. But these are enough to prove him right when he wrote, "The Sultan of Swat had a lot of the Canuck of Clout in him."

Whose body lay in state in the old Montreal Forum?

The funeral of hockey player Howie Morenz, known as the Stratford Streak, was held in the old Montreal Forum at centre ice on 11 March 1937. Fifty thousand people filed past the catafalque, and 250,000 Quebeckers lined the route to the cemetery. It attracted more mourners than any other funeral service in Canadian history to that point and probably since, as well.

Who invented the jockstrap and the goalie pad?

The athletic support for men, also known as the jockstrap, was invented by Joseph Cartledge of the Elastic Hosiery Company in Guelph, Ontario. He devised the support in 1920 and patented it in 1923, marketing it under the trade name Protex 13, according to Ken Lefolii writing in *Weekend,* 16 June 1979.

Goalie pads worn by hockey players are said to have been invented by a hockey enthusiast known as Emil "Pop" Kenesky of Hamilton in 1924. His handmade pads, modelled on cricket pads, were able to stop slapshots travelling at 145 kilometres per hour. Even in his 90s, he was making three hundred sets of pads a year. Kenesky Sports & Cycle of Hamilton, Ontario, offers a full line of sports gear, as well as training courses.

What is the greatest number of goals recorded in a World Championship hockey match?

In the World Championship hockey game played in 1949, Canada defeated Denmark 47–0. This is the most goals ever scored by both teams; as well, it is the most goals scored by any one team in a World Championship match, according to the 1975 *Guinness Book of World Records*.

Who in the role of King Lear declaimed, "Canada 6, Russia 5?"

That was the score of the final hockey game of the Team Canada–USSR Summit Series on Moscow ice on 28 September 1972. Paul Henderson's overtime goal brought the closely fought series to a fitting close. The words themselves were uttered by classical actor William Hutt.

Hutt was at the time playing the lead in a matinee performance for students of Shakespeare's play *King Lear* at the Stratford Festival. According to Richard Ouzounian, writing in "Taking a Final Bow," *Toronto Star*, 10 April 2005, "Hutt sensed the audience would all rather be elsewhere, but he soldiered bravely ahead as the mad king. Just before the famous storm sequence, Hutt heard in the wings that Paul Henderson had scored the decisive goal. He played through the scene with full passion, then, at the conclusion, turned to the people and simply said, 'Canada 6, Russia 5.' The crowd went wild."

William Hutt's impromptu remark is now enshrined in hockey fame and theatre history.

How long are NHL hockey players on the ice at any one time?

Most hockey fans are surprised to learn that the average hockey player during a National Hockey League game is on the ice for only 40 seconds at a time. That at least was the average in 2003. It may be even less today because the duration of the "sprint" is decreasing with the years. The "shift" of the average player in 1952 was two minutes. They had endurance in those days. Today they have strength.

The effect of duration on play was noted by Ken Dryden in his article "Saving the Game," *The Globe and Mail,* 27 March 2004. "Playing two minutes at a time, a player has to play a coasting-bursting style of game to save energy. You coast in the neighbourhood of the puck at most moments, then when there is an offensive chance or a defensive urgency, you burst. Playing 40 seconds at a time, you burst all the time. You play at a sprint. I remember little of high school physics, but I do remember: $F = ma$. Force equals mass times acceleration. So when a body that weighs 29 pounds more moves at a sprinting speed, the force of collision is significantly, dangerously greater."

In what years have Canadian athletes failed to win gold medals at the Olympic Games?

Canadian athletes are among the world's best, despite government programs that have inhibited and impeded their best efforts, especially at the Olympic Games.

There are both Winter and Summer Olympic Games. Canadian competitors won no gold medals at the Winter Games in 1936 (Garmisch-Partenkirchen), 1956 (Cortina d'Ampezzo), 1972 (Sapporo), or 1980 (Lake Placid). As well, Canada failed to win gold medals at the Summer Games in 1972 (Munich) and 1976 (Montreal). At these Games, Canadians earned silver and bronze medals in goodly numbers, but not one gold medal.

Sports nicknames

Some sports personalities have nicknames and monikers that are officially recognized in Canada's Sports Hall of Fame. Here are 12 such names of the old-timers.

Match the name with the nickname and the sport.

1. A.H. Fear	Dynamite	Hockey
2. Fred Taylor	Newsy	Hockey
3. Aubrey Clapper	Shotty	Football
4. Eddie James	Red	Football
5. Hawley Welch	Dit	Hockey
6. Richard Howard	Pep	Rowing
7. Edouard Lalonde	Cyclone	Football
8. Frank R. Leadley	Huck	Hockey
9. Leonard Kelly	Kid	Hockey
10. Levi Rodgers	Toe	Football
11. S.P. Quilty	Silver	Football
12. Hector Blake	Cap	Boxing

ANSWERS:
1. Cap, football; 2. Cyclone, hockey; 3. Dit, hockey; 4. Dynamite, football; 5. Huck, football; 6. Kid, boxing; 7. Newsy, hockey; 8. Pep, football; 9. Red, hockey; 10. Shotty, rowing; 11. Silver, football; 12. Toe, hockey.

What are ringette and floor hockey?

Ringette and floor hockey are popular, non-commercial, non-contact, fast-moving team sports.

Both ringette and floor hockey are modelled on ice hockey and were developed by Sam Jacks, a parks and recreational director of North Bay, Ontario. Recognizing that hockey has an appeal to youngsters and women as well as to boys and men, he devised these two team games. They are now so popular that there are national and international leagues, as well as many amateur teams in numerous countries.

Jacks developed floor hockey as early as 1936, but it was only in 1970 that it caught on in a big way. It is played by two teams of six players apiece, on a surface of wood or concrete instead of ice. There are no skates, sticks, or pucks. Instead players wear sneakers, wield wooden poles, and drive open-centred disks. Floor hockey is the only team game recognized by the Special Olympics. It was first played at this level at the 1970 Special Olympics Winter Games.

Ringette, sometimes described as "the little sister to hockey," is played on skates on ice. Like floor hockey, there are two teams, each with six players (one goalie, two defence, one centre, two forwards). A straight stick is used instead of a hockey stick, and a rubber ring in place of a puck. The game is organized on skill levels: Bunnies (learning to skate), C, B, A, AA, and AAA. There are local, regional, national, and international tournaments.

Both ringette and floor hockey have many players and fans nationwide. Competition and cooperation are both required in successful play. Both games have two features that render them superior—in some people's view—to hockey: no physical contact between players is allowed, and there is no professionalization, with its accompanying commercialization.

Maple Leafs or Leaves?

Why is the hockey team in Toronto called the Maple Leafs and not the Maple Leaves?

This question has long intrigued hockey commentators and fans of the game, though there is no record of any National Hockey League player showing interest. Steven Pinker, a Montreal-born cognitive neuropsychologist, asks the question in the context of the pluralization of word formations in his probing 1994 study *The Language Instinct*. It seems our internal sense of grammar and word formation distinguishes between common nouns and proper nouns (those derived from names), and our brains treat them differently: "As for the Maple Leafs," writes Pinker, "the noun being pluralized is not *leaf*, the unit of foliage, but a noun based on the *name* Maple Leaf, Canada's national symbol."

Who were Canada's Top 10 female and male athletes of the 20th century?

A survey conducted of newspaper editors and radio and TV broadcasters by The Canadian Press/Broadcast News produced lists of the top 10 female and top 10 male athletes of the 20th century. Here are the lists, in order of choice:

1. Nancy Greene	1. Wayne Gretzky
2. Silken Laumann	2. Gordie Howe
3. Barbara Ann Scott	3. Bobby Orr
4. Myriam Bédard	4. Lionel Conacher
5. Marnie McBean	5. Maurice Richard
6. Bobbie Rosenfeld	6. Donovan Bailey
7. Catriona LeMay Doan	7. Fergie Jenkins
8. Sandra Post	8. Mario Lemieux
9. Marilyn Bell	9. Larry Walker
10. Elaine Tanner	10. Gaëtan Boucher

This information comes from "Canada's Female Athletes of the Century," *The Globe and Mail*, 23 November 1999, and "Male Athlete of the Century," *The Globe and Mail*, 30 November 1999.

Were there any years the Stanley Cup was not awarded?

Yes. The Stanley Cup, the oldest trophy in professional sports in North America, was originally donated by Governor General Lord Stanley to encourage competition in hockey. It has been awarded to winning teams every year since the 1892–93 season, with the exception of two seasons.

The games were suspended in the 1918–19 season at the request of public health officials who were attempting to restrict the spread of influenza. The Spanish flu epidemic was responsible over a two-year period for the deaths of fifty thousand Canadians and 21 million people worldwide.

The season of 2004–05 was officially cancelled on 16 February 2005. The lockout of players lasted 154 days. Negotiations between the club owners of the National Hockey League and the players represented by the NHL Players' Association failed to reach a compromise agreement on a maximum team salary cap. Affected were 30 teams, 792 players, 1230 regular season games, and millions of hockey fans in North America. The cancellation called into question the parlous state of Canada's national game—highly commercialized, given to violent outbreaks, and "professionalized."

As one sports commentator suggested, the Stanley Cup went unawarded the first time because of influenza, the second time because of "affluenza." As former hockey star Ken Dryden wryly observed, "Canadians will have to decide whether hockey is a habit or a passion."

Indeed, the trustees of the Stanley Cup were encouraged by hockey fans to remove the cup from the control of the National Hockey League and award it, for one year at least, to a non-League team, perhaps a women's hockey team. For well or ill, this transfer did not occur.

What are the national sports of Canada?

Canadians are generally considered to be "good sports," wishing the world well. On 12 May 1994, the Parliament of Canada declared ice hockey the national winter sport and lacrosse the national summer sport.

Curling is the official sport of which province?

The official sport of the province of Saskatchewan is curling. Indeed, residents of the province have excelled in the sport and are probably responsible for its popularity across the country.

Where is there a Lacrosse Museum and Hall of Fame?

The Parliament of Canada recognized lacrosse as the country's national summer game. (And, as also noted earlier, hockey was similarly recognized as the country's national winter game.) There is no museum devoted to the game in Canada, but there is one in Baltimore, Maryland, next to Johns Hopkins University's Homewood Field. Its official name is the National Lacrosse Museum and Hall of Fame. *More Than a Game,* the video shown at the American museum, notes that the game was being played by the Huron Indians in the Thunder Bay area in 1636. A demonstration of the sport in 1834 in Montreal led to its popularity among non-Aboriginal North Americans. Lacrosse was Canada's undisputed national game until the phenomenal rise of interest in ice hockey in the 1920s.

What is the significance of Mile 3339?

There is a simple white marker in a farmer's field in the Township of Shuniah, northeast of Thunder Bay, Ontario. It was erected by the Ontario Ministry of Transport but it is privately maintained. It marks the point on the Trans-Canada Highway where the one-legged marathon runner Terry Fox collapsed. To raise funds for cancer research, Fox covered 5374 painful kilometres, more than half the distance from Halifax to his home in Burnaby, British Columbia. The official point of commemoration is the Terry Fox Scenic Outlook, some miles farther west. The words on the sign read: "Mile 3339 / Terry Fox's / "Marathon of Hope" / September 1, 1980." So the significance of Mile 3339 is twofold. First, young Terry Fox made a difference. Second, everyone may make a difference.

Which artist wrote and performed a song about Terry Fox?

Rod Stewart, the British soft-rock singer and performer, headed a benefit in Boston, Massachusetts, on 5 August 1989 to honour the memory of Terry Fox, the marathon runner who died at the age of 22 in 1981. Stewart wrote and performed a song titled "Never Give Up on a Dream." Royalties earned from the song are earmarked for cancer research.

What is the Fox 40?

Fox 40 is the brand name of the referee's whistle now sanctioned for use by all major sporting organizations. It was designed in 1987 by Ron Foxcroft, who now manufactures it through Fox 40 International.

"Fox" stands for Foxcroft and "40" stands for the age of the designer/manufacturer when he developed the plastic whistle. Foxcroft, a native of Hamilton, Ontario, and an enthusiastic sportsman, served as a basketball referee at McMaster University. He noted that the regulation pea whistle used to referee most sporting events was unreliable. For instance, it jammed when blown too hard—the "pea" lodged and the whistle failed to sound. Working with a series of prototypes, Foxcroft developed a plastic, pea-less whistle; its practicality and reliability were immediately recognized by sporting officials.

In addition to running Fox 40 International, Foxcroft served as president of Fluke Transport & Warehousing. The well-known trucking firm's motto is amusing: "If it arrives on time, it's a Fluke." One might add, "If it makes a loud noise, it's a Fox 40."

Which popular board games were devised by Canadians?

Some board games devised by Canadians are identified in *Canada Firsts*, written by U.S. consumer critic Ralph Nader (with research by Nadia Milleron and Duff Conacher). Here are a few of the games they name:

- Trivial Pursuit (introduced in 1979–81) by Chris Haney and Scott Abbott of Toronto.

- Yahtzee (introduced in the 1800s) by a wealthy Canadian couple on their yacht, hence they called it "The Yacht Game"; they sold the rights in the 1920s and the name was changed to the now-familiar Yahtzee.

- Balderdash (introduced in 1984) by Laura Robinson and Paul Toyne of Toronto.

- An Evening of Murder (introduced in 1986) by Max Haines, crime reporter.

- Supremacy (introduced in 1984) by Robert Simpson of Toronto.

- A Question of Scruples (introduced in 1985) by Henry Makow, writer and former professor in Winnipeg.

- Pictionary (introduced in 1986) by Rob Angel of Vancouver.

- Ultimatum (introduced in 1985) by Fred Bates of Hamilton.

These board and card games keep families and friends entertained during our long winter nights.

Arts and Letters

Was Sherlock Holmes a Canadian?

Enthusiasts of the Sherlock Holmes stories enjoy arguing strange theses and proving odd theories about the characters, such as whether Dr. Watson was five-times married, or whether Holmes was a Canadian. The latter notion stems entirely from the Canadian habit of adding the particle *eh?* to the ends of sentences. Holmes, it seems, uses the construction in a number of instances, notably in his first adventure, *A Study in Scarlet,* in which he says to Watson, "I might not have gone but for you, and so have missed the finest study I ever came across: a study in scarlet, eh?" The consensus is that Sherlock is as English as they come, but that may not be true of Dr. Watson.

Through foreign eyes

Delightful observations have been made about us and our country. Some appear below. Match them with the names of the famous observers (and the years of the observations).

1. Canadian girls are so pretty, it is a relief to see a plain one now and then.

   a. Rupert Brooke, 1913

2. Canada has held, and always will retain, a foremost place in my remembrance.

   b. Charles Dickens, 1842

3. But my impression is that they have all the faults of the Americans, and not their one lovely and redeeming virtue, "hospitality."

   c. Henry James, 1883

4. We are off, off into Toronto Bay (soon the wide expanse and cool breezes of Lake Ontario) ... Goodbye, Toronto, with your memories of a very lively and agreeable visit.

   d. Mark Twain, 1883

5. Niagara Falls is the most beautiful object in the world.

   e. Walt Whitman, 1880

ANSWERS:
1. d; 2. b; 3. a; 4. e; 5. c.

What is "La Maison aux pignons verts"?

That is the title, in French, of L.M. Montgomery's classic novel of child-hood, *Anne of Green Gables*. It was translated by Henri-Dominique Paratte and published in Montreal in 1986.

Does the name of a Canadian girl appear in J.K. Rowling's book "Harry Potter and the Goblet of Fire"?

J.K. Rowling's children's book *Harry Potter and the Goblet of Fire* is a popular work of fiction published in 2000. In July 1999, while working on the manuscript in Edinburgh, Scotland, the author received a letter about Natalie McDonald, a nine-year-old Toronto girl dying of leukemia who was comforted by the Harry Potter books. The letter was written by family friend Annie Kidder, who requested that Rowling correspond with Natalie by email. Rowling agreed but her email arrived one day after Natalie's death on 3 August 1999. Natalie's mother and family and friend Annie Kidder began to correspond with Rowling, and a transatlantic friendship developed. Unknown to Natalie's family and friends, Rowling commemorated the name of her young fan who did not live long enough to read a copy of *Harry Potter and the Goblet of Fire* by giving the name Natalie McDonald to a first-year student of Hogwarts School of Witchcraft and Wizardry. The full story of this incident was told by Brian Bethune, "The Rowling Connection," *Maclean's,* 6 November 2000.

First lines of six novels

Here are the opening lines of some novels. The titles of these novels and their authors are listed on the right. Match them.

1. There are some stories into which the reader should be led gently, and I think this may be one of them.

   a. Roberston Davies' *Fifth Business*

2. Here was the least common denominator of nature, the skeleton requirements simply, of land and sky—Saskatchewan prairie.

   b. Margaret Laurence's *The Diviners*

3. I don't know whether you know Mariposa.

   c. Stephen Leacock's *Sunshine Sketches of a Little Town*

4. My lifelong involvement with Mrs. Dempster began at 5:58 p.m. on the 17th of December, 1908, at which time I was ten years and seven months old.

   d. Hugh MacLennan's *The Watch That Ends the Night*

5. They are, I thought sadly, what they eat.

   e. John Metcalf's *General Ludd*

6. The river flowed both ways.

   f. W.O. Mitchell's *Who Has Seen the Wind*

ANSWERS:
1. d; 2. f; 3. c; 4. a; 5. e; 6. b.

How many painters were members of the Group of Seven?

This may seem a simple question, yet it is really a tricky one. The answer is that there were 11 members of the Group, which consisted of painters who jointly exhibited their uninhibited landscapes from 1920 to 1932 before disbanding, if you count the honorary founder Tom Thomson. But "Group of Eleven" lacks the traditional connotations of the number seven, which is considered to be magical if not mystical.

The initials of the original seven members are F.C., L.H., A.Y.J., F.J., A.L., J.E.H.M., and F.V. What are their full names?

Three more painters were later admitted to the Group. Their names are Casson, Fitzgerald, and Holgate. Supply their first names.

Why was Tom Thomson never a member of the Group?

ANSWERS:
Original members of the Group of Seven were Franklin Carmichael, Lawren Harris, A.Y. Jackson, Franz Johnston, Arthur Lismer, J.E.H. MacDonald, and Frederick Varley. Subsequent members were A.J. Casson, L.L. Fitzgerald, and Edwin Holgate. The inspiration of the Group's art was Tom Thomson, who died in 1917, three years before the Group formed. He is considered an unofficial member.

What is the setting of the world's first werewolf film?

Transylvania would be a reasonable answer, with a nod to the classic cinematic version of Bram Stoker's *Dracula,* starring Bela Lugosi as the king of the vampires. But a vampire is not a werewolf. Predating that classic is *The Werewolf,* the almost completely unknown movie shot in Canada in 1913 by the director Henry McCrae. He based it on the short story "The Werewolves," written by Henri Beaugrand and set in New France in 1706. It told (in 18 minutes) of a brand of cannibalistic Iroquois who camped at the mouth of the Richelieu River, south of Montreal. The Indians not only drank the blood and ate the flesh of their victims but turned into *loups-garous* (werewolves) during the process of their horrible feast, according to horror buffs Don Hutchison and Peter Halasz, who have described this rare, silent motion picture.

Who was the bombshell from Paris?

A publicist in Hollywood was the first person to call Fifi D'Orsay the "Bombshell from Paris." Truth to tell, the dancer—and star of vaudeville, Broadway, and Hollywood—never in her life visited Paris. She was French-Canadian, having been born Marie-Rose Angelina Yvonne Lussier in Montreal in 1904. When she was 16 and trying her luck as a dancer in New York, she adopted the stage name Fifi D'Orsay, which sounded so Parisian! She joined the comedy act of Gallagher and Sheen and then began to appear in Hollywood musicals, including *Young as You Feel* (1930) with Will Rogers, and even in a forgettable Monogram movie called *The Girl from Calgary* (1932). As she became too old to be a "bombshell," she made fewer and fewer movies, preferring to work in nightclubs as a singer and dancer. She made a comeback of sorts when Harold Prince cast her in her old role in the revival of *Follies* (1970). She died in Woodland Hills, California, in 1983, a movie legend.

Did Mary Pickford ever appear in a Canadian movie?

Mary Pickford, the silent-film star who enjoyed so much popularity with audiences and the public in the silent-film period that she was dubbed America's Sweetheart, appeared in 147 short films released between 1909 and 1913, and in 54 feature films released between 1913 and 1933, the year she retired. A filmography appears in Eileen Whitfield's appreciative biographical study *Pickford: The Woman Who Made Hollywood.*

All of these shorts and features were produced in the United States. Pickford never appeared in a Canadian-made movie. Yet, of special interest to Canadians is the fact that she was born in Toronto and made special arrangements with the Department of Citizenship to regain her Canadian citizenship before she died.

In one of her movies (and perhaps in two of them), she plays the part of a Canadian woman. She plays the role of an Eskimo lass in *Little Pal.* Set in the Yukon, the 1915 feature film is based on a short story by Marshall "Mickey" Neilan and was directed by James Kirkwood. Pickford plays an Inuit girl in a "dispirited style," according to one reviewer. The movie was greeted with dismay, her biographer Eileen Whitfield notes, perhaps because Pickford hid her well-loved golden curls beneath a long black wig.

One of Pickford's short films might have Canadian content and might be set in Nova Scotia. It is a 1910 film called *An Acadian Maid.* No description of its setting or action is known.

So the short answer to the question posed above is no. Mary Pickford never appeared in a Canadian movie. But she played at least one role identified with Canada. The plaque on the statue of Pickford raised in her hometown of Toronto describes her as "cinema's first superstar."

Who introduced sound to the movies?

Hollywood's first sound feature film was *The Jazz Singer,* starring Al Jolson and released in the fall of 1927. Charles Foster, a film historian, claims that the technical honours for this achievement could be awarded to three people in Hollywood at the time. There is Jack Warner, head of Warner Brothers, which released Jolson's movie. Louis B. Mayer, head of Metro-Goldwyn-Mayer, maintained that Douglas Shearer, a sound specialist in his employ, laid the groundwork. Allan Dwan, a producer at Warner, filmed a newsreel with sound for Movietone News in the summer of 1927, ahead of the movie. As Foster points out, all the contributors were Canadians, sound Canadians.

What are the 10 best Canadian films of all time?

There are various lists of the top 10 Canadian feature films. Three were compiled at 10-year intervals (1984, 1993, and 2004) by the Toronto International Film Festival Group, a charitable, cultural, and educational organization devoted to celebrating excellence in film and the moving image.

On 19 September 2004, the Festival Group announced the poll results for Canada's top films of all time. The poll was based on the responses of a group of one hundred filmmakers, programmers, and industry representatives from Canada and around the world. For the three polls, the Toronto International Film Festival Group asked critics, programmers, and industry professionals to compile a list of their top Canadian films. Many old favourites reappear on the list, as well as a handful of new features.

Here are the titles of the top films (with years of release and names of directors), arranged in declining order of importance, with several films tied:

Mon oncle Antoine (1971); Claude Jutra
Jésus de Montréal (1989); Denys Arcand
The Sweet Hereafter (1997); Atom Egoyan
Goin' Down the Road (1970); Don Shebib
Atanarjuat (2001); Zacharias Kunuk
Dead Ringers (1988); David Cronenberg
Les ordres (1974); Michel Brault
Les bons débarras (1980); Francis Mankiewicz
Le décline de l'Empire Américain (1986); Denys Arcand
Les invasions barbares (2003); Denys Arcand

You'll note that Montrealer Denys Arcand directed 3 of the 10 films, and that the list excludes documentary films and made-for-television movies.

Did Bugs Bunny visit the Klondike? Was Elmer Fudd a Mountie?

Bugs Bunny, the fast-talking hare, visits the Klondike in the 1959 seven-minute cartoon titled *Bonanza Bunny*. This cartoon introduces the character Blacque Jacque Shellacque, the French-Canadian answer to the cartoon character Yosemite Sam. Shellacque, who claims, "I'm the roughest, toughest, meanest, etc., Canuck in the Klondike," tries but fails to rob Bugs of his carats.

Bugs revisits the Klondike, where he again encounters Blacque Jacque, a popular villain with young audiences. In *Wet Hare* (1962), Bugs tries to take a shower "by a waterfall," but Blacque Jacque Shellacque wants all the water for himself. It also is seven minutes long.

Elmer Fudd, the fuddy-duddy cartoon character, plays a Mountie in *Fresh Hare* (1942). He fumbles his investigations with much muttering and stammering. According to film exhibitor Reg Hartt, "This is a great little film, but the ending is cut from current prints, as it features black folks."

What are the three most-acclaimed Canadian films of all time?

What a loaded question.

Nanook of the North is probably the most acclaimed Canadian motion picture of all time. It was set and shot in the Arctic and has as its subject the daily life of the Eskimo. What could be more Canadian than that? Directed by documentary filmmaker Robert Flaherty and released in 1922, its ambience was recreated in 1994 as *Kabloonak (Nanook),* which was directed by Claude Massot and starred Charles Dance and other fine actors.

Of contemporary films, two feature dramatic films that were written, produced, and directed by consummate filmmaker Denys Arcand rise head and shoulders above all the rest. The first is *The Decline of the American Empire* (1986). As film critic Gerald Pratley noted in *A Century of Canadian Cinema,* "The conversation is witty, sharp, funny, furious, bright and bitchy. The film is a triumph for the players and Denys Arcand. It brought him the recognition at home and abroad he so richly deserved after making many distinguished but less-noticed movies."

Arcand went on to produce its sequel: *The Barbarian Invasions* (2003). Pratley described it as one of "the truly great films of our time." He added, "It is nostalgic, bittersweet, and satiric yet wise about love and life, vice and virtue, politics and pretentiousness. It is all Arcand, with his humour, charm, and clear-minded intellectual expressionism. And behind it all, we can imagine his serious creativity, mixed with his spontaneous laughter and sense of enjoyment." The two films focus on the lives of a group of male and female university professors who meet for dinner and talk about sex and sociology, their personal relationships, and private fantasies.

Both of Arcand's films are Quebec films before they are Canadian films or American films, yet their appeal is universal. Both depict human relationships against the backdrop of American values and Western civilization with an affectionate yet critical regard.

Hollywood's brightest Canadians

Hollywood would still be Hollywood without its colony of Canadian actors, not to mention its producers and directors, but without them there would be fewer stars in the firmament above Los Angeles.

Below are listed 20 youngish acting talents and their birthplace, followed by a list of feature movies. Match performer with film.

1. Pamela Anderson, Ladysmith, British Columbia

   a. *Back to the Future*

2. Dan Aykroyd, Ottawa

   b. *Barb Wire*

3. Neve Campbell, Guelph, Ontario

   c. *The Black Dahlia*

4. John Candy, Toronto

   d. *Breakfast with Scott*

5. Jim Carrey, Newmarket, Ontario

   e. *Canadian Bacon*

6. Megan Follows, Toronto

   f. *The Center of the World*

7. Michael J. Fox, Edmonton

   g. *Eternal Sunshine of the Spotless Mind*

8. Paul Gross, Calgary

   h. *Ghostbusters*

9. Natasha Henstridge, Springdale, Newfoundland

   i. *Little Shop of Horrors*

10. Mia Kirshner, Toronto

    j. *Love Monkey*

11. Meg Tilly, Texada Island, British Columbia

    k. *Mars Attacks!*

12. Carrie-Anne Moss, Vancouver

    l. *The Matrix Revolutions*

13. Rick Moranis, Toronto

  m. *Murder Most Likely*

14. Mike Myers, Scarborough, Ontario

  n. *Relative Strangers*

15. Catherine O'Hara, Toronto

  o. *The Secret Life of Words*

16. Sandra Oh, Nepean, Ontario

  p. *Shrek*

17. Molly Parker,
 Maple Ridge, British Columbia

  q. *Sleep with Me*

18. Sarah Polley, Toronto

  r. *Under the Tuscan Sun*

19. Jason Priestley, Vancouver

  s. *Where the Wild Things Are*

20. Martin Short, Hamilton, Ontario

  t. *The Whole Ten Yards*

ANSWERS

1. b; 2. h; 3. n; 4. e; 5. g; 6. d; 7. a; 8. m; 9. t; 10. c; 11. q; 12. l; 13. i; 14. p; 15. s; 16. r; 17. f; 18. o; 19. j; 20. k.

Who are notable Canadian photographers?

There are innumerable Canadian photographers of national interest and international importance. They work as photojournalists and as art photographers.

Robert J. Flaherty took fabulous still photographs of the Inuit way of life in the eastern Arctic, as well as producing and directing the world's first feature-length documentary film, *Nanook of the North*.

Richard Harrington's photographs of the starving Padlimuk band of Inuit of the eastern Arctic led to their airlift to safety.

Yousuf Karsh's famous "bulldog" portrait of British prime minister Winston Churchill became a rallying point in the Second World War.

The Montreal photographer Robert Del Tredici risked life and limb to capture for a book-length album of still photographs the images of nuclear power production and weaponry.

Edward Burtynsky's "manufactured landscapes" capture the peculiar beauty of humans' depredations of nature in spectacular photographs, the basis of the feature-length documentary film *Manufactured Landscapes*.

There is that arresting photograph of John Torrington, the member of one of the Franklin expeditions to the eastern Arctic, frozen in the Arctic ice, taken by an unidentified photographer with the expedition.

Jeff Wall is identified with arresting and supersized photo-transparencies of living tableaux in art galleries.

The TIROS satellite on its flight over Earth captured the sole sign of life on the planet visible from space: the clear-cutting of timber near the logging town of Cochrane, Ontario, taken on 4 April 1961.

Who were "Your Eminent Residences" at the Stratford Festival?

Tyrone Guthrie, artistic director of the Stratford Festival, was wryly amused, upon his arrival at Stratford, to find in his theatrical troupe a "house," a "hut," and a "mews"—in the persons of talented actors Eric House, William Hutt, and Peter Mews. He addressed them as "Your Eminent Residences."

Which famous musician frequently misspelled his own name?

Glenn Gould's name and signature were quite unusual.

Recipients of letters from the recording artist found that he seldom bothered to write the last letter of his first name. When in haste he would sign his letters "Glen Gould." The signature looks odd. The family name is also misspelled.

Scholars have noted that at his birth, on 15 September 1932, the future pianist was registered "Glenn Herbert Gold." Although the family was Presbyterian, because of the anti-Semitic atmosphere of Toronto at the time, family members felt it wiser to spell the family name "Gould" rather than "Gold"—a name identified with European Jewry.

What is the country's bestselling magazine?

Maclean's is generally considered the country's bestselling publication, but it is not.

The six leading English-language periodicals in terms of issues printed are, in order of decreasing circulation, *Reader's Digest, Chatelaine, Canadian Living, Homemakers, TV Guide,* and *Maclean's.* That list was valid until 26 November 2006, when it was announced that the print edition of *TV Guide* would be replaced by an electronic version on the web. That gives *Maclean's* pride of fifth place.

Who was the world's first TV personality?

Joan Miller was the first person to appear on the world's first television program. Born in Nelson, British Columbia, and later an actress based in London, England, Miller was cast by BBC-TV as the presenter (or host) of *Picture Page,* its inaugural daily magazine-style program. It debuted on 2 November 1936. The show was immediately popular, and Miller was dubbed "the switchboard girl," because she "connected" the various guests who appeared on the long-running program.

Which Canadian's photograph appears on the Beatles' Sergeant Pepper's album?

That is a tough question unless you've read Charles Foster's well-researched book *Once Upon a Time in Paradise: Canadians in the Golden Age of Hollywood.* In 1967, the Beatles released their great *Sergeant Pepper's Lonely Hearts Club Band* album. No one was more surprised to find his photograph included in the collage of the album's cover than child star Bobby Breen. Born in 1927 in Montreal and raised in Toronto, Breen was an appealing youngster who could sing, dance, and act. Once his talent was discovered, he rode the wave of Hollywood's interest in child stars during the Great Depression and war years, appearing in a handful of movies, including *Let's Sing Again* with Eddie Cantor and *Hawaii Calls* with Canadian-born comic actor Ned Sparks. He remains an entertainer to this day, still wondering why the art director of the Beatles album included him along with occultist Aleister Crowley and other notables.

What are the myths of television?

The so-called myths of television are those of Mark Kingwell, a philosopher at the University of Toronto and a prolific essayist who contributes popular articles on design, technology, and social policy to newspapers and magazines.

There is an essay in his book *Practical Judgments: Essays in Culture, Politics, and Interpretation* titled "Fear and Self-Loathing in Couchland: Eight Myths about Television." The title is provocative (to the extent that it is meaningful), yet it does offer the reader an intellectual's organized response to some of the criticisms of the medium of television. Kingwell begins, "Because I have some critical things to say about television in what follows, I want to make it clear from the outset that I write as someone who believes television is a medium *worth taking seriously*" (emphasis in original).

Here are the points he makes, shorn of the arguments pro and con that support them:

1. Television is a neutral medium.
2. Television is controlled by individuals.
3. Television is democratic.
4. Television is all junk.
5. Television is responsible for the world's evils.
6. You can talk about television on television.
7. Intellectuals are right to discount television.
8. Television is beyond saving.

After making these points and offering contexts for them, Kingwell comes to the conclusion that they are all myths—and therefore untrue. This leads him to a further conclusion: "And thank god every day for print. Because I couldn't have said any of this on television. It took me more than eight minutes."

Who is Eilleen Edwards?

Eilleen Edwards is the birth name of the popular singer known as Shania Twain. Twain is her stepfather's last name. Eilleen changed her first name to Shania in 1991, and success as a composing, performing, and recording artist followed. Shania is said to be a woman's name in the Algonquian language. (The singer's adoptive stepfather was Ojibwa.) Nicholas Jennings, writing in "Overture," *Maclean's*, 3 December 2001, identifies Twain as "the highest-selling female artist in the history of country music."

Hit songs

Who wrote these hit songs? Match the titles with the songwriters.

1. "Both Sides Now" (1967)
2. "Four Strong Winds" (1966)
3. "Heart of Gold" (1972)
4. "My Way" (1974)
5. "Sometimes When We Touch" (1977)
6. "Sudbury Saturday Night" (1969)
7. "Suzanne" (1966)
8. "Universal Soldier" (1963)

a. Paul Anka
b. Leonard Cohen
c. Stompin' Tom Connors
d. Dan Hill
e. Joni Mitchell
f. Neil Young
g. Buffy Sainte-Marie
h. Ian Tyson

ANSWERS:

1. e; 2. h; 3. f; 4. a; 5. d; 6. c; 7. b; 8. g.

Walk of Fame

Here are the names of inductees into Canada's Walk of Fame. There is a star for each and every one of them embedded in the sidewalk of Toronto's entertainment district, a tradition established in 1998 along the lines of the long-established Hollywood Walk of Fame, which honours with bronze stars embedded in Hollywood Boulevard the stars of Hollywood's motion pictures. Canada's Walk immortalizes (in the words of the dedication) men and women from many walks of life, not just the movies, although the emphasis remains, it seems, on entertainers of screen and stage who have made their reputations south of the border. The names of these "immortals" appear below, with field of recognition and place of birth and/or hometown. The list includes those entertainers who were born here, and also those who were born elsewhere but were brought here when young and whom we claim as our own.

The latest inductees were announced in March 2007: Johnny Bower (hockey), Rick Hansen (athlete and activist), Jill Hennessy (television), Chad Kroeger (rock band Nickelback), Catherine O'Hara (comic), Gordon Pinsent (theatre), Ivan Reitman (film director), and Lloyd Robertson (journalism).

In your household, how many of these men and women (and some performance groups) are household names? Does it seem reasonable to include the late movie mogul Louis B. Mayer because he was raised in Saint Jean, New Brunswick? David Steinberg but not Stephen Leacock? Not the animator Norman McLaren or the poet/songwriter Leonard Cohen? Who else is missing? Give the organizers your nominees: feedback@canadaswalkoffame.com.

Bryan Adams, musician (Kingston, Ontario) 🍁 Paul Anka, musician (Deschambault, Quebec) 🍁 Denys Arcand, film director (Deschambault, Quebec) 🍁 Kenojuak Ashevak, painter (Ikirlsak, Nunavut) 🍁 Margaret Atwood, author (Ottawa, Ontario) 🍁 Dan Aykroyd, actor (Ottawa, Ontario) 🍁 Jean Béliveau, hockey player (Trois-Rivières, Quebec) 🍁 Pierre Berton, author (Whitehorse, Yukon Territory) 🍁 Scotty Bowman, hockey coach (Montreal, Quebec) 🍁 Kurt Browning, figure skater (Caroline, Alberta) 🍁 John Candy, actor (Newmarket, Ontario) 🍁 Jim Carrey, actor (Newmarket, Ontario) 🍁 Juliette Cavazzi, singer (Winnipeg, Manitoba) 🍁 George Chuvalo, boxer (Weyburn, Saskatchewan) 🍁 Cirque du Soleil, circus troupe (Gaspé, Quebec) 🍁 Michael Cohl, producer (Toronto, Ontario) 🍁 Alex Colville, artist (Toronto, Ontario) 🍁 Pierre Cossette, producer (Valleyfield, Quebec) 🍁 Toller Cranston, skater (Hamilton, Ontario) 🍁 David Cronenberg, director (Toronto, Ontario) 🍁 Hume Cronyn, actor (London, Ontario) 🍁 Céline Dion, singer (Charlemagne, Quebec) 🍁 Shirley Douglas, actor (Weyburn, Saskatchewan) 🍁 Jim Elder, equestrian (Toronto, Ontario) 🍁 Linda Evangelista, model (St. Catharines, Ontario) 🍁 Timothy Findley, novelist–scriptwriter (Toronto, Ontario) 🍁 Maureen Forrester, singer (Montreal, Quebec) 🍁 David Foster, music producer (Victoria, British Columbia) 🍁 Michael J. Fox, actor (Edmonton, Alberta) 🍁 Glenn Gould, musician (Toronto, Ontario) 🍁 Nancy Greene, downhill skier (Ottawa, Ontario) 🍁 Wayne Gretzky, hockey player (Brantford, Ontario) 🍁 The Guess Who, musicians (Winnipeg, Manitoba) 🍁 Monty Hall, game show host (Winnipeg, Manitoba) 🍁 Rex Harrington, ballet dancer (Montreal, Quebec) 🍁 Evelyn Hart, ballet dancer (Toronto, Ontario) 🍁 Ronnie Hawkins, musician (Huntsville, AK; Peterborough, Ontario) 🍁 Arthur Hiller, film director (Edmonton, Alberta) 🍁 Gordie Howe, hockey payer (Floral, Saskatchewan) 🍁 William Hutt, actor (Toronto, Ontario) 🍁 Lou Jacobi, actor (Toronto, Ontario) 🍁 Ferguson Jenkins, baseball player (Chatham, Ontario) 🍁 Harry Winston Jerome, sprinter (Prince Albert, Saskatchewan) 🍁 Norman Jewison, director (Toronto, Ontario) 🍁 Lynn Johnston, cartoonist (Collingwood, Ontario) 🍁 Karen Kain, ballet dancer (Hamilton, Ontario) 🍁 John Kay, musician (Toronto, Ontario) 🍁 Diana Krall, musician

(Nanaimo, British Columbia) ✴ Daniel Lanois, musician (Hull, Quebec) ✴ Mario Lemieux, hockey player (Montreal, Quebec) ✴ Robert Lepage, stage director (Montreal, Quebec) ✴ Gordon Lightfoot, musician (Orillia, Ontario) ✴ Rich Little, impressionist (Ottawa, Ontario) ✴ Guy Lombardo, bandleader (London, Ontario) ✴ Louis B. Mayer, Hollywood pioneer (Minsk, Russia; Saint John, New Brunswick) ✴ Lorne Michaels, producer (Toronto, Ontario) ✴ Joni Mitchell, singer (Fort McLeod, Alberta) ✴ Alanis Morissette, musician (Montreal, Quebec) ✴ Anne Murray, singer (Springhill, Nova Scotia) ✴ Mike Myers, actor (Scarborough, Ontario) ✴ Leslie Nielsen, actor (Regina, Saskatchewan) ✴ Bobby Orr, hockey player (Parry Sound, Ontario) ✴ Walter Ostanek, polka king (Duparquet, Quebec) ✴ Mary Pickford, actor (Toronto, Ontario) ✴ Luc Plamondon, musician (Saint-Raymond-de-Portneuf, Quebec) ✴ Christopher Plummer, actor (Toronto, Ontario) ✴ Ivan Reitman, producer (Komarmo, Czechoslovakia; Hamilton, Ontario) ✴ Ginette Reno, singer (Montreal, Quebec) ✴ Maurice Richard, hockey player (Montreal, Quebec) ✴ Jean-Paul Riopelle, painter (Montreal, Quebec) ✴ Robbie Robertson, musician (Toronto, Ontario) ✴ Royal Canadian Air Farce, comedy troupe (Montreal, Quebec) ✴ Rush, musicians (Toronto, Ontario) ✴ Barbara Ann Scott, figure skater (Ottawa, Ontario) ✴ SCTV, comedy troupe (Toronto, Ontario) ✴ Buffy Sainte-Marie, songwriter (Piapot Reserve, Saskatchewan) ✴ Mack Sennett, Hollywood pioneer (Montreal, Quebec) ✴ William Shatner, actor (Montreal, Quebec) ✴ Helen Shaver, actor (St. Thomas, Ontario) ✴ Wayne and Shuster, comedy duo (Toronto, Ontario) ✴ David Steinberg, comedian (Winnipeg, Manitoba) ✴ Teresa Stratas, opera soprano (Toronto, Ontario) ✴ Donald Sutherland, actor (Saint John, New Brunswick) ✴ Kiefer Sutherland, actor (St. Thomas, Ontario) ✴ Veronica Tennant, ballet dancer (London, England; Toronto, Ontario) ✴ The Tragically Hip, musicians (Kingston, Ontario) ✴ Shania Twain, musician (Windsor, Ontario) ✴ Jacques Villeneuve, race car driver (Saint-Jean-sur-Richelieu, Quebec) ✴ Jack Warner, Hollywood pioneer (London, Ontario) ✴ Fay Wray, Hollywood pioneer (London, Ontario) ✴ Neil Young, singer (Toronto, Ontario)

Odds and Ends

Is there a Sasquatch memorial in western Canada?

No, there is no memorial anywhere in Canada to the Sasquatch, the legendary or real hairy giant of the Northwest. However, a park that lies north of Harrison Hot Springs in the Interior of British Columbia, where the creature is said to have his haunt, is officially named Sasquatch Provincial Park. In the words of one travel writer, "The park's visitors are more likely to sight bald eagles, great blue herons, and mallards than they are to spot the legendary monster."

There are a number of memorials to the giant in the western United States, where the Sasquatch is known as Bigfoot. The biggest memorial is a 2.4-metre-high statue, carved from wood by Bigfoot enthusiast Jim McClarin, which stands at the junction of Highways 299 and 96 at Willow Creek, in northern California.

Where are you guaranteed to see Ogopogo?

Ogopogo is the aquatic creature said to inhabit the calm waters of Okanagan Lake, in the Interior of British Columbia. Few if any of the tourists who visit the Okanagan Valley in the summer will report spotting the serpent-like creature. But most of the tourists will see effigies of Ogopogo in Kelowna and Vernon, cities located on the shores of the lake.

You are guaranteed to see two Ogopogos—or two likenesses of Ogopogo—in the City Park in downtown Kelowna, British Columbia. The first is an effigy of the sea serpent with a green body and a red forked tongue that rises from the reflecting pond. The second is the image of the marine monster that looks down on the park from the height of the totem pole carved by Oliver Jackson in 1955 to mark the city's 50th anniversary.

In Vernon, Ogopogo takes the form of a green, serpentine fountain in Polson Park. In addition, between Kelowna and Vernon, on the shoulder of Highway 97, which overlooks Okanagan Lake, there stands an official marker erected by the Department of Recreation and Conservation identifying Squally Point as Ogopogo's home.

What are Father Lonergan's philosophical precepts?

Father Bernard Lonergan of the Society of Jesus was the leading theologian of the Roman Catholic Church in Canada. The University of Toronto Press has issued influential texts in a multi-volume edition of his collected writings. *Insight: A Study of Human Understanding,* first published in 1957, offers his transcendental precepts as to how one should live his or her life. There are five precepts, of which the first—"Be attentive"—is the fundamental one. The other four precepts are "Be intelligent," "Be reasonable," "Be responsible," and "Be in love."

What is the colour of your passport?

There is a colour code for Canadian passports.

The cover of your passport is green if you are a member of the Privy Council, a member of Parliament, a provincial premier, or a provincial cabinet minister.

The cover of your passport is red if you are a member of the diplomatic corps.

If you are none of the above, like the vast majority of Canadians, the cover of your passport is bluish-black.

How do you read your passport?

You can read your passport the same way a computer does.

Passports issued by Foreign Affairs Canada are described as machine-readable. They are based on standards issued by the International Civil Aviation Organization. Machine-readability contributes to the security of the document and to faster clearances through document checkpoints. Information in the 2005 brochure titled "Important Notice" issued by Foreign Affairs Canada offers the following interpretation of data on page two of your passport.

The first eight lines contain personal information and, together with a photograph, form the visual zone. The last two lines at the bottom of the page form the machine-readable zone, which repeats the personal information and passport details in a special format.

The machine-readable zone can also be read visually from left to right using this description:

Upper line
   a. Code "P." identifies the document as a machine-readable passport (2 characters)
   b. Code of Canada "CAN" as issuing country (3 characters)
   c. Surname and given names of passport bearer (39 characters)

Lower line

   d. Passport number (10 characters)

   e. Nationality of passport bearer "CAN" (3 characters)

   f. Date of birth (7 characters)

   g. Sex "M" or "F" (1 character)

   h. Passport expiry date (7 characters)

    The sequence and number of allowable characters for each field are specified in the international standards. The symbol · is used to fill spaces in fields that would otherwise be blank. The last numbers in fields d, f, and h, and the final number are check digits that are generated from a numerical equation to assure the accuracy of the information. Note that the information page has been laminated to prevent tampering and ensure durability.

A Clutch of Urban Legends

Is there an urban legend about Lake Louise?

There certainly is, and it is recorded in "The Gullible Tourist" by Thomas J. Craughwell in his collection *Urban Legends: 666 Absolutely True Stories That Happened to a Friend … of a Friend … of a Friend,* who sets the background to the story: "Lake Louise, near Banff, Alberta, is a remarkably deep shade of blue. The colour is so striking that it almost seems artificial." As the story goes, every year, on 22 September, the lake is drained, and the bottom of the lake is painted a vivid shade of blue. This accounts for the vividness of the colour.

Apparently, one summer an American woman who was a guest at the Chateau Lake Louise heard the tall tale from a lifeguard and decided to return two months later to watch the colouring of the lake. And that is what she did, with a camera and lots of film to record the event.

Is it an urban legend that Tim Hortons spikes its coffee with nicotine?

Yes, it is a legend. No, the Tim Hortons chain of coffee shops does not add nicotine to its coffee, doughnuts, or other baked goods.

Tim Hortons is the country's best-known chain for coffee and fresh-baked goods. "Always fresh" is the company's slogan. The outlets are "always open." The chain was founded in 1964 and has in excess of 2000 outlets across Canada, as well as over 140 locations in the United States. Its coffee is described as a "special blend," and the specific ingredients and preparation processes are a company-held secret.

The popularity of Tim Hortons' coffee probably generated the rumours that circulated—perhaps by enthusiasts for rival chains—that the company's products were addictive and that the ingredient responsible was nicotine. Why nicotine? It is highly toxic, even in small amounts, and is not permitted to be used as a food additive in either Canada or the United States.

No evidence of nicotine was ever found in the chain's coffee or baked goods. The amount of caffeine in the coffee is about the same as the level of caffeine in Starbucks or Second Cup brews. The urban legend was the subject of a CBC-TV *Disclosure* episode in February 2004.

Is there an urban legend about free Air Canada tickets?

One urban legend about Air Canada's free tickets has been making the rounds since the 1960s. Purportedly, the national airline decided to offer business-class travellers two tickets for the price of one. The idea was they would take their wives (presumably, the only business travellers at the time were men) along on their business flights. About 1000 executives took up the offer. A couple of months into the program, the airline's promotional department contacted the executives' wives. About 90 percent of them, when asked what they thought of the promotional package, answered, "What business trips? My husband never took me on any of his business trips."

What is the urban legend about the dog named Gellert?

"After the death of his wife, a fur trapper took his infant and his large sled dog and moved into a cabin high in the Canadian Rockies, miles from any town or homestead. While the man set and checked his traps, the dog guarded the baby." So explains Thomas J. Craughwell in his collection *Urban Legends: 666 Absolutely True Stories that Happened to a Friend ... of a Friend ... of a Friend.*

On his rounds, the trapper got caught in a blizzard, and it took him hours to get back to his cabin. "When he arrived, he found the door ajar. Cocking his rifle, he rushed into the house. To his horror, he saw the baby's crib overturned and no sign of the child. From behind the bed, crept the trapper's dog, its fur matted with blood.

"With a cry of anger and despair, the trapper shot his dog dead. Then the trapper heard the sound of his baby crying. He looked behind the bed and saw his son, safe and unharmed, lying on the floor. And sprawled beside the child was the body of a huge timber wolf, dead where the trapper's dog had killed it."

Craughwell explains that the story of Gellert is at least a century old and is widely told throughout Europe.

Does the American flag fly over the Centre Block on Parliament Hill on the Canadian two-dollar bill?
This is an urban legend that circulated in the United States. I first encountered it in 1997.

How many Americans have ever seen a Canadian two-dollar bill? How many Americans would find a two-dollar bill trustworthy, considering that such bills (known as "shinplasters") are shunned by most Americans? For that matter, how many Canadians have seen a two-dollar bill, which was replaced by the two-dollar coin in 1985?

An examination of the two-dollar bill reveals no sign that the Maple Leaf flag has been replaced by the Stars and Stripes.

Weather records

Mark Twain once said that everyone talks about the weather but nobody ever does anything about it. But truth to tell, nobody talks about the weather as much as does David Phillips, the Environment Canada climatologist who loves to amuse and bemuse us with stories about our nation's eccentric and extreme weather records. He once explained, "I always say there are 31 million weather experts in this country." Here are some Canadian extremes and records (to date), for the weather-wise.

Warmest temperature: 45 degrees Celsius—5 July 1937; Midale, Saskatchewan

Coldest temperature: minus 63 degrees Celsius—3 February 1947; Snag, Yukon Territory

Most rain: 6655 millimetres—Henderson Lake, British Columbia

Least rain: 61 millimetres—Rea Point, Fort Simpson, Northwest Territories

Most sunshine: 2537 hours—Estevan, Saskatchewan

Least sunshine: 949 hours—Stewart, British Columbia

Greatest snowfall: 1433.0 centimetres—Glacier National Park, British Columbia

Least snowfall: 28.6 centimetres—Rea Point, Fort Simpson, Northwest Territories

Greatest average wind speed: 33.7 kilometres per hour—Cape St. James, British Columbia

Greatest calm: 4.4 kilometres per hour—Summerside, Prince Edward Island

All wet

Why should you be all wet to celebrate the second Sunday in June?

ANSWER:
On 8 June 2003, Heritage Canada designated the second Sunday in June as Canadian Rivers Day. It draws attention to the Heritage Rivers System, which consists of the 30 or more rivers that are part of the National Parks of Canada. Obviously, the way to celebrate a river is to be "all wet"—to sail it, swim it, fish it, paint it, or photograph it.

Dollars and cents

The purchasing power of the dollar has been in steady decline over the decades. If $1.00 buys a chocolate bar in 2007, it bought five chocolate bars in 1967. Chocolate bars may be better, bigger, or bitterer than they once were, but the principle holds. Here is an illustration of the decline in value of the dollar.

In 2007, a dollar is worth a dollar (that is, $1.00).
In 1997, it was worth $1.16.
In 1987, it was worth $1.53.
In 1977, it was worth $3.14.
In 1967, it was worth $5.82.

Note how the dollar's purchasing power has diminished more than 500 percent in four decades. Scary.

Spiritual beliefs

Reginald Bibby is a leading pollster who examines mores and customs, as well as political activity. "Bibby's poll shows that Canadians do indeed embrace an array of spiritual beliefs alongside traditional articles of faith. A third of us believe in astrology, and more than half (57 percent) are fairly sure ESP exists. Two-thirds think there's life after death, more than believe in either heaven or hell. Slightly more than 31 percent consider it likely that we can communicate with the dead, although 46 percent think we can do so with the spirit world. It seems a glaring contradiction that the number of people who believe we can communicate with spirits is 50 percent greater than those who think we can talk to the dead—especially since millions of Christians pray daily to saints, all of whom are dead." These are the findings of sociologist Reginald Bibby as quoted by Brian Bethune, "Maclean's Poll 2006," *Maclean's,* 1 July 2006.

What would Alberto Manguel deposit in his own national time capsule?

Alberto Manguel, essayist and anthologist, responded to the challenge of an exhibition in Paris called "Visions of the Future" to develop his own national time capsule to recall for far-future generations the dreams of contemporary Canadians. He wrote about this in "Ghosts of the Future: Unborn Dreams," *The Globe and Mail,* 28 October 2000. Here is what he said he would preserve for posterity:

> I'd like to think that the list would be wonderfully eclectic: the petroglyphs in the Saskatchewan prairie that hold messages yet to be deciphered; the tent in Auschwitz where the stolen belongings of the inmates were kept and which was known as "Kanada"; Pierre Trudeau's brave Constitution for a country he believed should stand firmly on its own; the failed Finnish project of Sointula that attempted to set up a socialist society in a coastal village in British Columbia; Margaret Atwood's cautionary novel *The Handmaid's Tale;* the perfect reading space of Toronto's Metro Library, one of the strongholds of our collective memories; the all-encompassing theatre of Robert Lepage, redefining the roles of the actor and the audience; David Suzuki's repeated warnings of future ecological devastation; Norman Bethune's work in China, foreshadowing the concept of *Médecins sans Frontières;* the 1999 Nunavut Act that holds in these desperate times an almost utopian promise that might just be fulfilled.

What would you place in *your* personal time capsule?

Phone home

What happens if you dial the telephone number 1 (800) O CANADA?

If you dial the number 1 (800) 622-6232 between 8:00 A.M. and 8:00 P.M. Monday to Friday, it will connect you with Service Canada, a department maintained by the Government of Canada to answer general queries about work and training related matters, tax and passport details, and so on.

The service is also accessible on the internet at www.servicecanada.gc.ca. Its FAQs (frequently asked questions) are well worth examining. The government's main website is www.canada.gc.ca.

Writing to Santa

If you write a letter to Santa Claus, he will write back to you. This service is brought to you and yours courtesy of volunteers at Canada Post. Santa's address is:

Santa Claus
North Pole H0H 0H0
Canada

For more information, check www.canadapost.ca/santascorner.

12

Laughing Matters

Psst, have you heard the one about ...?

Yes, Virginia, there is a Canadian sense of humour.

Just read the stories of Stephen Leacock. Or turn on the radio and listen to Rex Murphy. Or switch on the television and watch *Royal Canadian Air Farce*. Or laugh as the richly talented Rick Mercer discusses current events.

Remember, the Second City troupe originated here, as did Mark Breslin's Yuk Yuk's comedy cabaret.

Now let me tell you some of my favourite jokes, anecdotes, and stories. There are 10 of them, some historical, some modern. All of them are Canadian classics.

Laugh along with me ...

1. Mounted Police

The classic story told about the Royal Canadian Mounted Police took place before the turn of the 19th century, during the days when the newly created force was still known as the North West Mounted Police. The incident in question occurred in present-day Saskatchewan, along the Montana border.

An entire regiment of U.S. cavalry accompanies over two hundred Cree to the border, where they are met by a single Mountie. The American commanding officer looks around with surprise and dismay. "Where's your escort for these dangerous Indians?" he asks.

"He's over there," answers the Mountie, pointing to a fellow constable tending their two horses.

2. Saskatoon

Two English women are crossing Canada by train. At a brief stop in Saskatoon, the older woman turns to the younger woman and says, "I wonder where we are."

The younger woman replies, "I have no idea, but I will find out."

She steps onto the platform and spots the dispatcher. "Excuse me, could you tell me where we are?"

"Saskatoon, Saskatchewan," he replies.

She boards the train, and the older woman asks her, "Well, where are we?"

The younger woman replies, "I still don't know. It's obvious they don't speak English here."

3. W.L. Mackenzie King

A classic story involves Prime Minister Mackenzie King and R.B. Bennett, leader of the Opposition. The story is based on an incident that occurred in the House of Commons in 1928 but seems not to be part of the official proceedings.

Bennett was baiting King: "I would like to know what the prime minister would think," Bennett asked, "if he went into his garden in the morning to pick pansies or violets and was confronted by six naked Doukhobors."

Without a moment's pause, Mackenzie King rose and replied, "I would send for my honourable friend the Leader of the Opposition."

4. Royal visit

It was the official duty of Camillien Houde, the ebullient, bilingual, and controversial mayor of Montreal, to welcome King George VI and Queen Elizabeth to his city on 18 May 1939 and accompany them on their drive through the streets of Montreal in an open car.

The king and queen were delighted to see such large and enthusiastic crowds, and so was Houde. He turned to the king and said, proudly, "You know, your Majesty, some of this is for you."

5. Elizabeth and Philip

Not long after the royal wedding in 1947, Princess Elizabeth II and Prince Philip, Duke of Edinburgh, toured Canada. One evening they dined on humble fare in a lumber camp in the wilds of northern Ontario.

They were served a hearty meal, and when the dinner plates were collected, before the serving of dessert, the waitress serving Prince Philip leaned over to him and said, "Save your fork, Duke. You'll need it for the pie."

6. Essay on elephants

Four students from four countries—Britain, France, the United States, and Canada—were asked to write an essay on the elephant.

The British student titled his essay "Elephants and the Empire."

The French student naturally called his "*L'amour* and the Elephant."

The American student gave his essay the title "Bigger and Better Elephants."

And the Canadian student, after much head scratching, titled his essay "Elephants: A Federal or a Provincial Responsibility?"

7. Multilingualism

Q. What do you call someone who speaks three languages?
  A. Multilingual.

Q. What do you call someone who speaks two languages?
  A. Bilingual.

Q. What do you call someone who speaks only one language?
  A. English Canadian.

8. Newfie joke

Q. What's black and blue and floats in the bay?

A. A Mainlander who tells Newfie jokes.

9. Crossing the road

Q. Why does a Canadian cross the road?

A. To get to the middle.

10. As Canadian as possible

Details are scarce but, apparently, in the early 1960s, the producers of a CBC radio show *This Country in the Morning* held a write-in contest that required listeners to complete the following statement: "As Canadian as possible …"

Radio listener E. Heather Scott won the contest. She completed the statement by adding the words: "under the circumstances."

Farewell!

Here are ways to say farewell in both official languages, in two of the Native tongues, and in Esperanto. Match the words of farewell with their respective languages.

1. Adiau!   a. Algonquian

2. Adieu!   b. English

3. Assutnail!   c. Esperanto

4. Goodbye!   d. French

5. K'gah waumin meenwauh!   e. Inuktitut

ANSWERS:
1. c; 2. d; 3. e Northern Quebec; 4. b; 5. a Cree farewell.

Acknowledgments

I am grateful to the editors at Penguin Canada, notably Helen Reeves and Jennifer Notman, for reminding me that I could and should research and write this book; Tracy Bordian, who handled the production; and copy editor Judy Phillips, for her careful work. Some of the boldly stated national facts and figures are not factoids but distillations of information found in the pages of the *Canadian Global Almanac 2005*, an almanac that I once edited. I also used the 2006 and 2007 editions of the *Pocket World in Figures*, issued annually by *The Economist*. It supplied rankings arranged under more than one hundred headings and also "country profiles" for close to fifty major countries of the world. I acknowledge the assistance of my researcher, the late Mary Alice Neal, and special research librarian Philip Singer. Thanks also to Simson Najovits for agreeing to our "debate," which has taken place in person and now in print. No book of mine is complete without an acknowledgment of the many contributions of my wife, Ruth.